Collecting
Poole Pottery

Robert Prescott-Walker

Francis Joseph
ISBN 1-870703-63-4

Acknowledgements

Grateful thanks are due to the combined efforts of a number of people who helped with the production of this book. Robert Prescott-Walker has taken the principal lead and he has thoroughly researched the subject of Poole Pottery despite moving to New York. We made a great deal of use of the Internet over this period, thanks largely to the effort of John Folkard who typeset this book. I would also like to thank John Clarke of Art Deco Etc for providing a superb collection for photography and helping with valuations, and Cottees Auction House of Wareham who provided additional photographs.

Also, of course, Trevor Leek who as usual did an excellent job with the photography.

Francis Joseph, Publisher

ISBN 1-870703-63-4

Published by Francis Joseph,
5 Southbrook Mews, London SE12 8LG

Photography: Trevor Leek. Additional photographs Cottees of Wareham

Typesetting by E J Folkard Print Services, 199 Station Road, Crayford, Kent DA1 3QF

Contents

Foreword

This book has come about for a number of reasons, not least the recent and current interest in the post-war wares produced at the Poole Pottery. The post-war wares epitomise the changes in contemporary British fashion, taste and society, and are heralded as examples of such in the many exhibitions and books concerning the period which have appeared over the last few years. This renewed interest, however, specifically in the wares of Poole Pottery, stems as much from the early collectors of such ware, many originally sparked by the exhibitions and publications of the early 1980s, as from the current interest being shown in the post-war period. For my part, I undertook this book thanks largely to my friendship with probably the longest standing collector of Poole, who has amassed one of the largest private collections covering the whole history of the company, namely John Clark.

John and I first met on a damp and chilly morning at a Newark fair almost twenty years ago. Sharing what appeared to be distinct similarities in terms of taste and ideas concerning certain aspects of late nineteenth and twentieth century British ceramics, we struck up a friendship that is still very much alive. It is John's collection, parts of which have already been exhibited and photographed for books and magazine articles, as well as being filmed, that form the majority of the illustrations in this book. I am, needless to say, very grateful for his patience and resilience, both of us having had to move, open, unpack, pack and replace innumerable boxes (the reserve collection) from the cellars and attic, during the days when his house was invaded by several guests in order to photograph his collection.

That there is even as much interest in the history of the Carter Poole Potteries, their tiles, architectural wares, sculptural wares, the ornamental and tablewares, is in no small measure due to the knowledge of the former Poole Pottery archivist, Leslie Hayward. Leslie would freely give his time to deliver numerous lectures for whom ever asked him as well as writing numerous articles on the subject. The initial few years of the Club magazine would have been very thin without his lengthy historical articles. For years and years the only reference work, well researched that it was, was the Jennifer Hawkins book. This was, however, seriously lacking, as far as collectors were concerned, in illustrations of the wares. This gap was filled with the publication of the Leslie Hayward book, edited by Paul Atterbury, in 1995.

Given the earlier works in this field, what I have tried to add is a historical context to the story of the Pottery, highlighting whenever possible the significance of surrounding social, economic and political concerns. Inevitably, events outside the walls of the Pottery played an important part in shaping its direction and development, two of the more obvious events being the First and Second World Wars. How the managers and supporting staff steered the pottery through such events depended on numerous factors such as the personalities involved, short term and long term planning and market research. Perhaps one of the most important issues was being able to keep the balance of the commercial side of production in line with that of the promotional or individual studio exhibition wares.

The longevity of the Poole Potteries, initially under the direction of the Carter family, aided with a strong supporting team, and later through the persistence of new managers and young designers, can only be seen as a testament to the happy and convivial working environment under which ever single worker made their own contribution.

Introduction

To some degree, it could be said that Poole Pottery owed its success to the fact that it was not located in or amongst the somewhat precocious and introverted Potteries of Stoke-on-Trent. As outsiders there was almost certainly a feeling of unfettered freedom and of experimentation, probably due to their remoteness and being largely out-of-sight-and-out-of-mind. To many within the Potteries and elsewhere the wares produced by Poole were considered initially as insignificant, akin to several other 'outsider seaside potteries', of which there were many, for obvious reasons. Their wares were to a certain extent bright, colourful, playful and amateurish, the designs on many of the 'gift wares' and even their commercial ranges owing much to their marine locality.

When not obviously influenced by their immediate surroundings the surface pattern and shape designs of Poole were heavily dependent on the apparently never-ending input of the many artists and designers who were either working for or commissioned by Poole Pottery. This again was something many within the Potteries considered an unnecessary expense, certainly in terms of the freedom and support given to those who worked at or with the Poole Pottery by the management.

From a technical stand point, Poole were always highly individual and innovative, often seeking the latest mechanical devices to aid production. No other firm during Poole's life-time produced in-glazed wares on such a commercial scale. Poole & Co were the second firm to install the revolutionary Dressler continuous firing tunnel kiln and the first pottery to have four such kilns installed, Bourne & Co at their Denby works in Derbyshire coming a close second along with Pilkington's Royal Lancastrian Works.

In the potteries of Stoke-on-Trent when artistic input was required, the artist or designer was expected to stay very much within 'traditional' or 'acceptable' lines associated with the pottery by which they were employed. Even here the artistic input, with a few exceptions, was not recognised or promoted in any way, in fact the reverse was usually the case. On the rare occasion when an individual designer or artist was recognised it was only with reluctance that the name of the designers was used. The exception to this being the name of Clarice Cliff whose work for Wilkinson's was promoted, as never before or indeed since, her name appearing as part of company's trade mark in larger letters than that of the company. In this instance such promotion was used by the managing director of the pottery, Colley Shorter, as a deliberate marketing ploy, with great effect. Such high profile marketing was soon being copied by a few others within the industry but only those with sufficient funds and the gumption to take up the ideas.

At Poole, it mattered little 'who' was individually responsible for each and every piece or design, as artistic input was encouraged from the thrower, the painter/paintresses and even the management. The person who devised the original concept would often be attributed with the work although the end result might have differed considerably from his or her concept. The boundaries of attribution become distinctly blurred in the later 'Craft Studio' wares. The recent tendency to 'label' and 'categorise' certain wares with certain designers/paintresses is the result of misplaced research and writings by authors on much of twentieth century ceramic and design history, where the objects and select individuals become more important than the overall approach and working of the pottery concerned, as well as being taken out of context by other cultural factors. Paintresses' script marks, seen on the bases of much pottery, were either meant as indicators to enable rates of pay or 'piece rates' to be calculated, something that those in the Poole Studio tried to avoid, or indicators of work that might need to be referred to for some adjustments.

This approach is one of the many factors associated with Poole Pottery throughout its history that distinguishes the working spirit and exceptional nature of the wares that were produced, right from the very inception of the Art pottery wares at the turn of the century through to the present. That is not to say that there have been some lean years over the last century but there have been relatively few of them.

What becomes more apparent after a closer look at the history of Carter firm and wares produced under the Carter umbrella, is the importance of the tile and architectural business to the fortunes of the firm. Tiles in particular from the late nineteenth century right through to today have become inextricably linked with cultural developments related to health, cleanliness and status, as well as economic and political issues, whether coal miners strikes, building booms or government building regulations. Tiles have played a far greater and more significant role in the history of ceramics and the ceramics industry than many authors have previously acknowledged, tiles being hived off and treated as a secondary and separate industry. This is not surprising however, as even in the industry they were often regarded as such.

At Poole one of the hidden qualities that is and always has been so important is the 'craft' of pottery and the unique skills involved in the process. It is the conscious awareness of the balance needed between retaining such craft skills and making use of mass production methods and the use of machinery, that has helped to keep Poole in a unique niche amongst rival potteries.

Recognition of the essential need to keep a balance between the commercial product and the studio or limited production runs of exhibition quality wares is another underlying yet vital requirement found throughout the history of the Poole Potteries. The need for such a balance is perhaps more obvious in the ornamental and tablewares of the Poole Pottery but there was just as much need on the tile and architectural side. At the White Works and Architectural Pottery it was the high profile decorative hand painted panels, artistic individual tile series and Della Robbia style decorative works that overshadowed the more mundane 'white tile'. However, it is the more commercial plain off-white tiling anonymously covering the walls of hospital corridors, operating rooms, lavatories, banks, hotels, bathrooms, kitchens and boiler rooms that were produced in their millions, that swelled the factory's coffers and should not be forgotten.

Standardisation of the tablewares through the introduction of the Streamline shape combined with the surface glaze effects of the Two-tone range, brought about a significant advance in the commercial viability of the pottery, bringing on-line the capabilities of high volume mass-production to an International market. At the same time the firm was able to make use of low-skilled labour to produce artist inspired and designed wares for true industrial production. This was something that had first been talked about at any length just prior to the First World War at the Bauhaus and later reiterated and discussed through various British institutions concerned with the relationship between Art and Industry. It was left to American manufacturers unhindered by historical precedence and 'tradition' to truly take-up the possibilities that standardisation held. That it took until the late 1930s in Britain to provide tangible items, be they designed by Susie Cooper or John Adams, for the augmentation of a closer relationship between Art and industry is perhaps par for the course. That the consumer and the manufacturer should lose sight of those achievements so quickly after the Second World War, instead pandering to the fanciful and short lived fashion styles of the 1950s and 1960s is our loss. In terms of ceramic production at least the modified Streamline shape was able to offer a vestige of what was deemed 'good design' for the consumer.

Another significant reason for the longevity of the Poole Pottery was it's ability to balance the production of the essential high volume mass-produced wares with the 'high-end' limited Studio or exhibition type wares. Whilst the latter expensive wares were essential in promoting and creating a demand for the former, it was, after all, the far greater financial returns from the volume production wares that supported the pottery. To this day much the same parity exists with the Studio wares, Collectors Club pieces and special editions in relation to the retail wares as seen in the shops and factory shop.

The one-off Studio wares are sought-after often purely because they were produced in relatively limited numbers, compared to full scale mass-production, but in just sufficient numbers and over a long enough period to make them locatable and therefore potentially available to be supplied to collectors. The 'rare' pieces being the trials, one-off's (usually experimental colourways, etc), exhibition pieces and special commissions, then becoming usually the most prized and valued. Recently a one-off trial vase, from the hand of Guy Sydenham in the 1970s Atlantis range of wares, must have left the ebay Internet auction seller somewhat bemused when it sold for $1,035, some 21 bids later, to a UK buyer having started at a derisory $5.00. Little did the seller know the significance of that impressed triangular mark!

It is interesting to see that today several pottery firms are deliberately exploiting the 'rarity', 'limited' production run and 'special or exclusive' pieces, as part of their day-to-day marketing strategy, Moorcroft pottery being amongst the leaders in this field. Poole Pottery themselves have developed this strategy in recent years, albeit with a relatively small turnover when compared to its overall commercial production figures.

Unlike potteries such as Shelley or Wilkinson, Poole did not pursue the path of high profile promotion and advertising. Poole Pottery throughout much of its history has often had paintresses giving demonstrations at its London shows, exhibitions or in the department stores with special displays. Today a visit to the Poole Pottery visitor's centre will reveal much of the current processes in the making of Poole Pottery, with a wide variety of demonstrations, many unchanged since the centre opened in the 1960s, (Established due to the high numbers of visitors since the 1940s who were becoming distracting). Poole advertised fairly frequently in the monthly trade journals but their adverts, if anything, had a subtle understated visual appeal, warm and homely, as opposed to the brash and vibrant contemporary look of some pottery adverts.

If there is one thing that should be gleaned from twentieth century British ceramic production it is that artistic or designer enterprise and expression when competently directed, with sympathetic and appreciative understanding, can make a marked and extremely valuable contribution to the whole direction, input and spirit within a company. Sadly, all too often in the Stoke-on-Trent Potteries in the twentieth century the story has been one of short-lived artistic input and merit, with little competent support or guidance.

The general tendency amongst many authors on ceramic and even design history has been to look at the objects and/or the designers plucked out of their surroundings. In such circumstances, devoid of any contextual relationship and understanding of the social, economic and political factors that might have had some bearing on the object or designer, it is difficult to fully appreciate and understand the place of the product within society. Previously authors have been keen to point to industry being 'hampered by tradition' as well as an 'uneducated public', which largely miss the point. Industry, by its nature, in an effort to exist amongst competition locally and from abroad, will produce whatever is demanded of it, production being directed by the costs of the end product to the consumer in the face of fellow competitors. Gone are the days when specific industries, such as the tile and architectural industry, could be a largely self-regulating concern with standardisation of products and co-operative or 'mutually beneficial' federations and associations to look after its members interests, both at home and abroad. Whatever the edicts of the 'good design' lobby or quiz committees, or the efforts of the government backed industry associations and councils in promoting 'good design', it is always the 'end consumer' that is of final concern to the manufacturer. Hampered by such a vast wealth of historical styles, patterns, nationalistic or emblematic associations, the buying public in Britain can only ever be served by producing a plethora of wares in innumerable styles or reducing all of those styles, patterns and designs down to their basics and producing a limited range of disassociated wares. In the end, whether the wares are deemed 'good design' or not matters little to the buyer who buys, for example, floral patterned tea wares because they like them and will use them.

Chronology

1855   Patent Architectural Pottery established in Hamworthy (later known as the Architectural Pottery).

1861   T. W. Walker's Patent Encaustic and Mosaic Ornamental Brick and Tile Manufactory established on the East Quay Road, Poole, by James Walker, formerly chief technician of the Architectural Pottery.

1873   Jesse Carter (1830-1927) acquired control of James Walker's works, the latter having run into difficulties and been declared bankrupt. The works apparently being titled Carter & Co.

1880   Purchase of part of the St George's Works, Worcester, Jesse Carter's part being named the St George's Tileworks.

1888   St George's Tileworks now owned by Carter, Johnson & Co.

1892   St George's Tileworks records cease.

1881   Ernest Blake (born in 1856-1883), Charles (born 1860-1934) and Owen (born 1862-1919) joined the family firm. Only two years later Ernest Blake died of rheumatic fever.

1890s   Edwin Page Turner joins Architectural works along with his half brother James Radley Young who arrived in 1893.

1895   Jesse Carter bought Patent Architectural Pottery, which had been producing hard bricks and floor tiles since 1855. Floor tile production was concentrated there leaving the Poole factory free for the production of glazed tiles and faience.

1896   William Carter Unwin, sculptor and modeller, joins company.

1900   The Art Pavements and Decorations Company was incorporated. The business was founded in 1859 as Degrelle Houdret & Co.

1901   Jesse Carter retires leaving Owen in charge of the artistic and technical side while Charles looked after the administration and business side. Another factory at Hamworthy, formerly used for the manufacture of ultramarine blue, was bought by the company and converted for making white glazed wall tiles (hence the name it become known as "White Works") and later coloured tiles.

1905   Charles Cyril Carter (1888-1969) – eldest son of Charles Carter joined the company.

1906	London offices established in Essex Street for the sale and contracting of tiles run by Arthur Owen Carter (1874-1956) (son of Alfred Carter, the elder brother of Charles and Owen) and assisted by Charles Cyril Carter.
1908	Carter and Co was registered as a joint stock company Ltd by shares. Roger (1890-1959) and Henry Carter, younger sons of Charles Carter, joined the firm.
1912	London branch was registered as a separate company taking up the title of Carter and Co, London, Ltd. having moved to 29 Albert Embankment. (A terrazzo department under Mr. R G Robinson was extended to include jointless flooring – sold under the name of "Laterite".)
1913	A continuous gas-fired Dressler tunnel oven for the firing of glazed tiles was built at "White Works". At the time there was only one other Dressler-type tunnel oven in existence in the country, that belonging to J H Barratt and Co, Ltd, Stroke-on-Trent, (Barratts were acquired by the Carter group in 1928.).
1914	Association with the Omega workshops until in 1919 with the closure of the works.
1917	Benjamin Evelyn Elford appointed to the board having previously been the company secretary.
1919	Owen Carter died. Charles Cyril Carter joined the board taking on the responsibility of running the Hamworthy floor tile works until 1921.
1921	Carter, Stabler and Adams was formed as a private company to develop the pottery work in which Cyril Carter and James Radley Young had been interested, Harold Stabler (1872-1945) and John Adams ARCA (1882-1953) who was managing director until his retirement in 1950, were partners. Truda Carter ARCA (1890-1958) was responsible for much of the design work.
	Cyril Carter become responsible for the domestic and ornamental wares, leaving Roger, his brother, to officiate at Hamworthy.
1926	Jesse Carter died at the age of 96.
1927	Roger and Henry Carter left the firm for personal reasons. A Williamson tunnel oven was installed at the Architectural Pottery. works and the whole works was largely rebuilt. A second Dressler tunnel oven was also installed in the "White Works."
1928	Charles Carter retired. Carter & Co Ltd. was registered as a public company with R. E. Elford, C. C. Carter, A. O. Carter and Herbert Carter (chairman of Art Pavements) as directors. Art Pavements and Decorators Ltd. and J. H. Barratt (1927) Ltd. joined the group.
1931	The tiling department of Art Pavements and Decorators was transferred to Albert Embankment as a result of joining the group in 1928.

| 1932 | The Marbolith Flooring Co Ltd. was taken over by Carter and Co London Ltd. and the jointless flooring section transferred to this company. |

1932   The Marbolith Flooring Co Ltd. was taken over by Carter and Co London Ltd. and the jointless flooring section transferred to this company.

1934   Charles Carter died at the age of 74.

The Terrazzo department at the Albert Embankment was transferred to the Art Pavements.

1937   The "White Works" were extended and a third Dressler kiln installed.

1938   John David Carter ARIBA AADipl., the second son of Cyril Carter joined the company.

1939   A L Crampton Chalk CA(Con) and S Goddard Watts FIPA, were appointed directors.

1945   Harold Stabler died. Roy T Holland appointed works manager.

1947   Benjamin Elford, and Herbert Carter retire. Cyril Carter elected chairman and David Carter appointed a director.

Arthur Owen Carter retires after 41 years managing the London office. H. R. Hidden takes over as the new London office manager.

1948   Hartlington Supplies joined the Group.

1949   The terra cotta and faience production was transferred to A. P. works, Hamworthy, leaving the Poole site free for the production of Poole Pottery.

1950   John Paget Bowman appointed director. Barratt passage kiln built. John Adams retires. Lucien Myers appointed managing director. Claude Smale appointed as designer but only for six months. Alfred Burgess Read RDI, was appointed to replace Smale as head of the design unit responsible for both the Tileworks and the Pottery.

1952   A branch office was established in Dean Street, Manchester. R Campbell and Sons join the Group.

1954   Ronald George Cole MSMA, appointed director.

1955   William David Cash-Reed appointed director. Guy Stringer appointed managing director of Carter Tiles.

1956   Tunnel kiln built at the "White Works" for bisque,

1958   Robert Jefferson appointed designer. The name Hartlington Supplies Ltd. was changed to Carter Tiles Ltd. and the assets of the Poole tile works were taken over by this company, leaving Carter and Co Ltd. as a holding company having no direct concern with manufacture.

1963   Lucien Myers left. Roy Holland becomes managing director and Tony Morris joins the firm.

Cyril Carter resigns from the Carter, Stabler & Adams board. After which the name changed to Poole Pottery.

1964   Pilkingtons Tiles Ltd. of Manchester who became the parent company of the Tileworks. Factories in Manchester, South Africa and Australia.

Cyril Carter finally retires aged 75 having spent 60 years with the firm.

1965   Robert Jefferson leaves.

1966   A second tunnel kiln built on the Floor Tile factory.

1969   Guy Stringer leaves Carter Tiles.

1970   Trevor Wright appointed as works director

1971   Entire Pilkington's Tiles Group purchased by Thomas Tilling Ltd.

1976   Roy Holland retires leaving Trevor Wright to become managing director. Guy Sydenham leaves Poole.

1979   Crafts Studio winds down.

1983   Bone China body introduced for gift wares

1992   Management buy-out leaves Peter Mills in charge and Poole, once again, an independent company.

1995   New Poole Studio established. Poole Pottery Collectors Club established.

2000   Poole Pottery move into new premises. Poole Pottery ceases manufacture of ware at the Quayside works which is then demolished at the end of the year to make way for factory outlets with housing above.

Founding of the Factory

The early years 1850s-1921

That the town of Poole should be associated with pottery is hardly surprising considering the vast local deposits of fine clay in the immediate area, not to mention the excellent facilities for transporting raw materials and/or finished products from the Port. During the eighteenth century regular consignments of the finest Dorset white ball clay were shipped from the port, much of it destined for the Staffordshire Potteries.

Larger and more established businesses either grew from what had once been a small practice, such as a country pottery, or in response to demand. The latter is the case for the Poole Pottery as we know it today, the demand during the mid to late nineteenth century for architectural and garden ceramics having moved on from merely being the domestic requirements of the local population.

How Jesse Carter and the story of the Poole Pottery came about is largely due to a business diversification and, as is often the case, fortuitous knowledge.

Jesse Carter was the part owner of a flourishing ironmonger and builders' merchant's business based in Weybridge, Surrey, due West of London. It would appear that Jesse Carter probably knew of the T. W. Walker Patent Encaustic and Mosaic Ornamental Brick and Tile Manufactory, Poole, run by James Walker, through the purchase of tiles and similar wares for the Weybridge business. Whether at that early stage Jesse knew that James Walker was a spiritual brother, (both devoted members of the Plymouth Brethren) is hard to say. Whatever the case, Jesse Carter most certainly would have known of the failing circumstances of Walker's business, as a consequence of purchases for the Weybridge business, and by two notices of sale by auction of the premises and stock being announced, the first on 11th January, 1866, followed by another in 1869. By 1873, when Walker was declared bankrupt, Jesse would have had plenty of time to consider the viability of taking on the business. Whatever his reasons, Jesse became the new owner of the Patent Encaustic and Mosaic Ornamental Brick and Tile Manufactory founded in the early 1860s, shortly after Walker had been declared bankrupt, and moved his family to Percy House, 20 Market Place, Poole.

One of Jesse Carter's first actions was to retain the services of James Walker to run the pottery, as Jesse had little knowledge of technical processes required to run the pottery. However, by 1876 discrepancies were found in the accounts and Walker was dismissed. The Pottery kept going although on very rocky ground, managing in the process to survive a fire in the newly erected lime kiln. Jesse was having little success in selling the wares produced at the pottery during much of the 1870s, his rival across the quay, the Architectural Pottery at Hamworthy being far more successful. Jesse tried to expand, buying the St George's Patent Brick, Pottery and Terra Cotta Works, Worcester, from D. W. Barker in 1880. This did not prove successful; only eight years later a partner had been brought in by the name of Johnson and by 1892 the St George's Tile works, as it was renamed, ceased to exist.

All the while, however, Jesse was making considerable progress at his Encaustic and Mosaic Ornamental Brick and Tile Manufactory, opening a London office in 1878 at 24, Featherstone Buildings, Holborn. Some major names in the tile business, including Wedgwood, were feeling the competitiveness of Jesse's firm, with agents complaining that not even they could buy tiles cheaper than Jesse was selling them. By 1881 with demand for his Poole tiles increasing Jesse brought in his three youngest sons into the business. Charles and Owen working on the pottery side while Ernest Blake undertook the book keeping in the London office, although Ernest was to die of rheumatic fever only two years later. Charles took on the responsibility for the administrative side while Owen contributed to the production and decorative side of the firm.

During the 1880s Carter & Co started to become a major force in the tile and architectural ceramics business, with very healthy order books for shop frontages, and a wide variety of floor and wall tiling schemes from plain geometric and encaustic to mosaic faience and glazed embossed. There was particular demand for Carter's pictorial mural tile panels initially within the town and surrounding area, but this shortly became national and even international. Little is known about the artists responsible for executing these murals during the 1880s but by the 1890s Carter's had employed Edwin Page Turner and his half brother James Radley Young both of whom were to make significant contributions to the artistic standards of the pottery. Even before their arrival, however, the company had found winning ways, being awarded the silver medal for 'Superiority in Workmanship and Materials' at the Building Trades Exhibition of 1886. Further awards, in the form of a Prize Medal and a Star certificate, were gained in 1891 from the Society of Architects.

The enthusiasm and demand for Carter & Co products did not occur by chance nor indeed was it entirely due to the excellence of the product. As has previously been mentioned, demand for decorative architectural materials and garden ornaments had grown considerably during the late nineteenth century, much of the demand created by numerous recently published books on the subject of house decoration. Books such as Charles L. Eastlake's *Hints on Household Taste*, published in 1878 and *The House Beautiful* by Clarence Cook, published in 1881, led the way towards a new fashion for 'do-it-yourself' interior design and styling. This fashion evolved as a consequence of the increased wealth of the burgeoning industries and growing international trade which filtered profits to a growing middle and upper middle class. Houses and their adornment became status symbols of new wealth and style, and in turn created further business opportunities for importing goods to fulfil demand as well as in the creation of merchandise with which to adorn and embellish the home. Firms such as Liberty were born from such beginnings, initially established to import Oriental goods sold in warehouses near London's docks and then developing into a high street retail outlet, making it more convenient for shoppers to select from an ever increasing range of goods old and new.

Until the 1860s, the decoration and adornment of the family home had been the prerogative of the man of the house, and his task was usually greatly eased by relying on inherited goods to furnish the home. With the advent of more readily available industrially produced wallpapers, fabrics, linen, furniture, tiling, etc, together with the ever increasing choice from various manufacturers, not to mention the imported goods on offer, the whole process of home decoration not only became more of a fashion statement but also became something far more time consuming. This is when the woman of the house began to take charge of the decoration of the home. Carter & Co were part of this new burgeoning industrial growth supplying floor tiling, wall tiling, wall tile schemes, tiled fire surrounds, pictorial panels, terracotta garden wares, etc.

Carter also realised the virtue of local patronage, developing contracts in the town of Poole and its local environs. The business of local patronage was almost certainly helped by Charles being elected to the Poole Town Council in 1888 as well as his being elected Mayor for a term. To this day, there are dozens of buildings in Poole and the surrounding area and as far as Birmingham, where one can see examples of the firm's output. The next development was to gain wider national and international recognition and this Carter & Co achieved through entering national exhibitions, such as the trade exhibitions discussed earlier, but also through general industrial exhibitions. This path was to prove of particular benefit in years to come.

Such was the success of the company that by 1895 they bought out what had once been their rival business, the Architectural Pottery Company, to be followed by the acquisition of an ultramarine blue manufacturers across the road from the Hamworthy Architectural Pottery in July 1901, later to be named the 'White Works'. These two purchases, in many respects, marked the arrival of the Carter company as a major force in the tile, ceramic architectural and related wares field, very much amongst, if not above, the likes of Doulton & Co., Lambeth, Maw & Co., Jackfield, Minton, Hollins & Co., Stoke-on-Trent, Wedgwood, Etruria and Woolliscroft & Son. Stoke-on-Trent. Carter's were now able to locate specific departments to certain sites. The newly acquired 'White Works' was devoted to the mass production of everyday, functional white tiles, which were very much in demand in the rapidly flourishing hospitals throughout the country. The Hamworthy works had been turned over to the production of floor tiles and the main East Quay works produced the decorative tiles, terracotta and faience.

The tiles themselves in terms of design were much like those of their competitors, with many single tile or fireplace panel designs showing the prevalent stylistic influences of the day. Art Nouveau stylised floral designs were moulded in low-relief and occasionally tube-lined, and there were stylised floral repeat designs and border tiles. The trade catalogues published by the various tile manufacturers in the years after turn of the century often showed little innovation, one catalogue looking much like another.

To add to the professional staff of Turner and Radley Young, William Carter Unwin joined the firm as chief sculptor in 1896, being responsible for the figurative modelling of the architectural faience. One of his important contributions was in the training of Harry Brown as his assistant who went on to produce some significant work for the company.

The next stage in the development of Carter & Co resulted in the foundation of an entirely new and separate business that was to become known as the Poole Pottery and involved the production of ornamental and tablewares. This highly significant development was due to Owen Carter and his interest and experimentation with glazes and handcraft techniques, in particular his love of lustre glaze effects.

Carter's would almost certainly have been aware of the publicity, status, financial benefits and general acclaim that followed the involvement of the Doulton Lambeth pottery with the Lambeth School of Art in the late 1860s, and the subsequent development of Doulton's own Doulton Lambeth Studio in the 1870s. When Carter & Co bought the rival firm, the Architectural Pottery, they soon learned of the numerous blank tiles that had been supplied to a certain William de Morgan, although by the late 1870s (therefore twenty years before Carter's involvement) de Morgan had started to make his own tiles. The association between Poole and de Morgan continued until at least 1905, as there are bowls and dishes decorated by William de Morgan with impressed marks, Carter, Poole, and dated to 1904, one example is a bowl in the Victoria & Albert museum, which had once belonged to the de Morgan family.

During the 1890s Owen Carter began experimenting with glaze effects, in particular lustre glazes, undoubtedly influenced by the work of de Morgan who was the pioneer in this field, but also by the lustre designs executed at Maw & Co, after designs by Lewis F Day, on tiles and vessels and perhaps also the work of the Burton Brothers at the Pilkington Pottery, Manchester. Owen worked very closely with the recently appointed glaze technician from Stoke-on-Trent, Alfred Eason, who was almost certainly responsible for the development of lustre glazes on tiles and decorative pottery along with James Radley Young. Young had recently rejoined the Poole pottery in 1906 following the establishment of his own pottery in Haslemere, Surrey, where he experimented for five years with functional and ornamental wares. All was now ready for the development of a new range of wares that would form the basis for the now renowned brightly coloured floral, abstract and animalistic designs, using a red earthenware body.

The new range of mainly lustre wares, along with other experimental glaze effects, were used on vessels, candlesticks, dishes, vases, jardinières, and bowls, not to mention the tiles and tile panels, and were designed by both Owen Carter and James Radley Young. These wares were often applied with insects, fish and reptiles, much in the manner of Continental majolica pottery and some of Mark V. Marshall's designs for the Doulton Pottery, Lambeth, during the 1880s. In the Poole Pottery Collection are several pieces of lustre ware with colours ranging from a red/gold lustre through to green, silver and black, ruby, blue, orange and purple. It appears from these and other known pieces, along with archive records, that

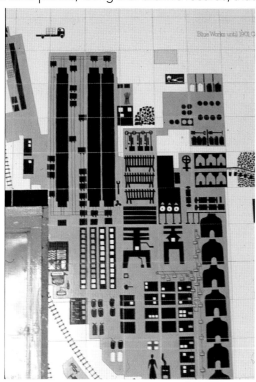

these wares were mainly made between 1900 and 1906, although some wares were still being made and exhibited until 1918 (British Industries Fair), a year before Owen Carter's death. Lustre tiles, which had initially been available as early as 1896, continued to be made into the 1930s. Such was the quality and effectiveness of the Carter lustre wares they frequently received praise in contemporary journals.

It should perhaps be remembered that this period from the turn of the century through to World War One was a time of experimentation within all aspects of the pottery industry, from the processes of manufacture and types of body, through to surface decoration and glaze effects. It was certainly helpful that public demand for 'artistic' wares heightened the search for new, better and unusual types of ware. Behind the scenes in the pottery itself there were also many major improvements in the process and making of the wares. One of the longest surviving, time consuming and most arduous of the processes was the firing of the ware. The solution to the problem was found with the invention and development of the Tunnel oven, which was then added to with further

Part of a large screen printed tile panel, dating from about 1959, depicting the mechanical and general making processes involved in the making of tiles in the White Tile Works. One can easily make out the three long Dressler tunnel kilns, and tracks for the trolleys, the clay presses on the right with flint kilns to the far right and the decorating and making shop below, with it's overhead conveyor belt.

developments such as the Top Hat kiln and Circular oven, this new technology taking days rather than weeks to complete the firing of an object. The end of the traditional bottle oven, which took some six to eight weeks to fire from placing the wares to emptying the kiln, was inevitable, although it took until the clean air act of the 1950s for it to actually happen.

Carter & Co with innovation and experimentation firmly established within the pottery decided to install a Dressler continuous firing tunnel oven in 1913, in an effort to cope with demand, specifically for white tiles destined for hospitals, government buildings, hotels, etc. That this Dressler tunnel oven was only the second ever such kiln to be built, the first being installed at the tile firm of J. H. Barrett & Co Ltd, in Stoke-on-Trent, showed something of the innovative and entrepreneurial spirit of the Carters. At 120 feet long, the tunnel oven needed to be housed in very large building, allowing extra space at either end for the introduction and extraction of the kiln trolleys.

Carters, along with many tile producers, suffered as a result of the war, which greatly limited production, but also the loss of staff. It was only due to the inventiveness of Owen Carter and James Radley Young that some sort of production continued, sporadic though it was. The remaining staff and kilns were turned over to the production of portrait plaques with images taken from photographs (The image was burnt into a light sensitive gel a few millimetres deep that coated a master tile, creating graduated layers according to the depth of light and shade on the photographic film. From the master, once the gel had hardened, a copy was made and developed into a mould from which numerous tiles could then be made. A majolica or pigmented glaze would then be poured and painted onto the tile, the deepest areas becoming darkest.) Perfume bricks and fire-lighters both made of an absorbent body which could then be filled with scented oil or paraffin were also produced.

James Radley Young's experimental work, however, was to prove the next important development for Carter & Co, laying the foundations for the highly successful brightly coloured wares of the 1920s and 1930s. Radley Young had been modelling some of the large pots requested by Liberty, which were produced between 1906 and 1910, but he had also started to make some unglazed hand-thrown vessels which he decorated with chevron and line bands or scrolling bands in manganese brown oxides. The shapes he used were based on ancient Moorish and Mediterranean originals, of simple form, the surface being deliberately left unfinished. Young particularly liked the

Early Carter, Stabler and Adams red earthenware jugs designed by J. Radley. Young (top two lines) and Erna Manners (bottom two lines). Studio Yearbook, 1922. This is the type of ware shown at the early trade shows such as the British Industries Fair.

idea of these wares being left in their natural state, showing the working method of throwing, rather than the smoothed over artificial appearance of similar 'craft' worked wares aping the perfection of mass production of industry. As a further development, Young produced two tin-glazed lines of ware, one with simple scattered floral motifs and another with horizontal and/or vertical blue lines, occasionally with floral motifs, that become known as Blue Stripe Ware. The Carter & Co British Industries Fair stand, 1921, was completely full of these wares along with the a few figurative models and two roundels by Phoebe and Harold Stabler. This fair marked the departure of the old and a new beginning.

With the search for more work to keep the ovens firing Carter & Co must have been very pleased and willing to help Roger Fry and his cohorts of the Bloomsbury group in the Omega workshops. This association, although relatively small in terms of output, played a part in laying the foundations not only for the frequent external involvement of artists and designers in the production of Poole Pottery but more importantly it gave an artistic input that was to affect future ornamental wares. Roger Fry, Vanessa Bell and Duncan Grant came to Poole to try their hand at throwing but it was Roger who showed the greater aptitude. Before long he was making prototype dinner wares, tea and coffee sets, vases and bowls, as well as tiles. In 1916 Roger spent a great deal of time visiting Carters & Co whilst working on the new commission to decorate Lalla Vanderville's flat, working on a complete dinner set decorated in black, dull yellow, green or purple glazes. We have already seen such an external influence through the lustre work of William de Morgan. The highly expressionistic and colourful designs of Vanessa Bell, Roger Fry and Duncan Grant together with the naivety and charm of their wares, made between 1915 and 1918, left their mark on the 1920s Poole Pottery designs to come.

At the same time as the association with the Bloomsbury Group but on the tile and sculptural side of the business, another artist, Joseph Roelants, was also to contribute in much the same vein to the improvement of the artistic output of the company. Jozef (anglicised to Joseph) Roelants arrived in Poole from Belgium in 1914 as one of many refugees. Shortly after this, he and fellow countrymen began to work at Poole Pottery. By 1917, Roelants had painted two series of tile designs, Dutch figures and Dutch boats together with executing several figurative sculptures, all of which were exhibited in the 1917 British Industries Fair, held in the Victoria and Albert Museum. Roelants tile designs and figures were very much in keeping with the freedom of expression and vibrancy found in contemporary Post-Impressionist paintings and which were also reflected in the work of the Omega Group. Roelants is also known to have carried out designs on bowls and other vessels, which like his tile designs were all executed by in-glaze painting, also known as Delft, a technique of which his countrymen where well aware.

It has been suggested that the Belgian refugees, Roelants amongst them, may have introduced the Delft technique to Poole Pottery but it would appear more likely that this decorative technique was introduced by Alfred Easton, who probably brought the idea with him from Minton where he had previously worked. Certainly, Easton and James Radley Young had developed the two tin-glazed lines of ware, Blue Stripe and scattered floral by 1914, it seems before the arrival of Roelants.

On a stylistic note the early pre-war Blue Stripe wares were, in the main, rather heavy in appearance, the colours used were particularly strong and the designs somewhat harsh and bold. The design often seems to overpower the shape, although the shapes themselves were, more often than not, heavy in terms of visual appearance and often in terms of weight. The few post-war pieces that were made up to about 1924 have an altogether far more harmonious look to them, the shapes are less exaggerated and flamboyant, whilst the designs have become bolder, covering more of the surface of the pot but in sympathy with the shape. It also helped that an increased colour palette was being used, much of it far more muted than previously. Perhaps the most significant change was to the designs themselves, many still based on the pre-war James Radley Young designs, which were then modified by Truda Adams and her female paintresses. This is where the wares of the Omega Group, their greater freedom of expression and bolder use of a wider range of colours, started to take effect.

The post-war unglazed wares again show more sympathetic surface patterns, bolder and more confident, on shapes modified by Truda Adams. The previously used small scattered floral sprigs become bolder and less numerous, with a far greater use of colour, all the rims having a repeated blue dash motif. It would also appear that the paintresses might have been given a slightly freer hand, and many of the post-war sprig designs may have originated from the paintresses themselves.

One of the most obvious technical differences in these pre- and post-war wares was the use of different bodies. The pre-war wares were in the main made from a semi-stoneware, more akin to a high-fired earthenware, which had a pale grey appearance seen on the foot. The wares made by the Bloomsbury Group used much the same body. The unglazed wares were hand thrown using a coarse terracotta-like body normally used for making tiles and were often extremely thin. The post-war Blue Stripe and floral decorated wares were either formed of a darker grey semi-stoneware or red earthenware body, the latter forming the basis of the future wares after this transitional period. The unglazed post-war wares used a high-fired terracotta coloured body and were often glazed on the interior.

That all this change and experimentation could take place was in part largely as a consequence of the War or rather the restrictions on what could and could not be made, together with the drop in demand for tiles and architectural wares due to the suspension of building work. The wares of James Radley Young had evolved largely out of need to fill a gap in production but as a result initiated the production of ornamental and functional wares at Poole that was to make the name of Poole Pottery known throughout the world.

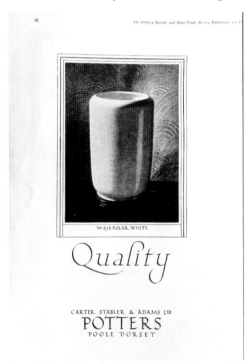

Carter, Stabler and Adams advert from the 1937 Pottery Gazette and Glass Trades Review Directory and Diary. The image and graphics used say much about the image and customer being sought after.

Carter, Stabler & Adams

The Art of Pottery 1921-39

The first decade of the twentieth century saw the firm foundation of the Poole Pottery but the next ten years can be seen, in many ways, as the most important and significant period in the history of the pottery, during which the ground work for the pottery's ultimate success was laid. Although initiated due to circumstance, namely World War One, the development of ornamental wares to run alongside, yet separate from, the tile and architectural business, enabled the Poole Pottery to become a complete enterprise producing highly affordable and well-designed wares for the public.

By 1910, Cyril Carter, Charles' son, was working for the family firm at their London office in Essex Street, under Arthur Owen Carter, Alfred's son, who was in charge of the office. Cyril was responsible for developing all the tiling contracts and it was largely due to his diligence and hard work that Poole Pottery reached the heights that it did by the beginning of the war. When the demand for tiles waned due to the halt of all building programmes, Cyril was put in charge of the Hamworthy floor tiles works, before moving onto what would be his most significant contribution to the pottery, the ornamental and decorative wares. Roger, Cyril's brother, took over from him at Hamworthy and around the same time Benjamin Evelyn Elford was appointed to the board having been company secretary.

The next stage in this transformation was the input of artistic ideas and skills linked with continued experimentation and technological improvement. This development was forced on the Carter family through the sad death of Owen Carter in 1919. Owen who had been in ill-health for some months, had been the driving force behind the artistic and technological developments at Poole, making the company a major force in the industry, and would be a difficult person to replace.

It was two years after Owen's death that the company, through the efforts of Charles and Cyril Carter, was able to find a solution to their problems and a new direction at the same time. It was decided to continue along a similar vein to that on which Owen had been concentrating, namely the ornamental and decorative wares, but to promote them more vigorously, with a view to them being a separate highly commercial and, if possible self-sustaining venture under the umbrella of Carter & Co. To this end, two new partners were brought into the fold, Harold Stabler and John Adams, and a new company was launched in 1921 under the title Carter, Stabler & Adams. At least this is how the new advent of the new venture has been relayed down to us over the years. In retrospect, I would be more inclined to say that 'four' new partners joined the firm, as Pheobe Stabler and Truda Adams, the wives of those previously mentioned, made a just as significant, if not more so, input into the pottery as their partners. Truda Adams (later Carter after 1930 having married Cyril Carter) in particular, made an enormous contribution in terms of design but also in the training of many of her colleagues over her nearly 30 years working for the company. There is much still to be researched about Truda's contribution to Poole, as well as several other fellow female artists and designers.

Harold Stabler was a well-known and talented artist and craftsman, having trained within the William Morris inspired Arts and Crafts Movement. He exhibited a multitude of works in diverse materials through out his formative years, becoming a teacher at the Royal College of Art and later at the Sir John Cass Technical Institute. Stabler's involvement with the British Institute of Industrial Art and the Design and Industries Association from 1915 was to prove invaluable to Poole Pottery for many years to come both as a source of commissions from his fellow members, but even more so as a source for promotion and recommendation. Indeed, Harold's contribution to the development of the Pottery is far less tangible than that of John Adams, for example, but none the less significant. Harold was able, through his connections in London, the DIA and other major institutions to which he belonged, to play a highly important promotional role behind the scenes. It was Harold who persuaded several graduate students, many from the Royal College of Art, to contribute, in some form or other, to the designs and production at Poole Pottery. In many respects, Harold and John Adams saw the occasional yet continuing contributions from external artists as a means of adding to the then current, often controversial, arguments concerning the links, or rather lack of them, between Industry and Art. Something that Poole could not be accused of, in fact quite the reverse, the company often being held-up as an example of how such associations could work.

Without getting too involved in the fascinating contextual issues and arguments of the relationship between Art (for Art read 'expression of beauty') and Industry (read 'standardisation'), good and bad design and the conjecturing of the various institutional bodies, government and independently backed, it is none the less interesting to see the position of Poole Pottery wares in this debate. Poole Pottery wares rank amongst the select craft-skills based 'Art wares' or 'Art Pottery' of the type advocated by those wishing to promote the virtues of an English style harking back to the Jacobean times, of the simplicity of honest craft work and design. The wares produced at Poole cannot be said to be based on limitation of shapes to a few standard mass-produced shapes with fast unskilled applied surface decoration, in fact quite the reverse. During this period, indeed throughout the history of the Pottery, with the exception perhaps of some of the tea and dinner wares, the production at Poole has been based on highly skilled and costly processes of production and decorative surface design, with the aim of selling to a limited market section. This hardly fitted comfortably within the 'fitness for purpose', simplicity and plainness of form and economy of decoration advocated by the Design Industries Association (DIA).

This argument between advocates of the need for better designed wares and surface decoration through the employment of more designers in industry versus the industrial response that they (industry) knew their own market place and what it required, was most active from 1918 through to the 1930s. There was genuine concern during this period regarding the competition from imported cheaper foreign goods, coming from Japan, Germany and other European countries, and also from the cheap mass production of everyday items made by back-street firms who had sprung up over-night to make a quick profit by flooding the market. Trade journals during this period had frequent articles from both sides of the divide, extolling "The Place of the Designer in the Pottery Industry", this the title of an article in the Pottery & Glass Trade Record by Arthur Finch in November 1924. In the early 1920s the example of the Carter, Stabler & Adams partnership was often heralded and illustrated as the right direction for other pottery manufacturers to follow. The 'example' being perhaps more related to the employment of designers at such a high level within a company and with an obvious management strategy to recognise the importance of design and the designer within the production process and ultimately, rather than necessarily, the wares. It should be said that, as I mentioned earlier, such arguments and articles were largely as a result of personal opinion and taste, and therefore subjective in terms of the 'type' or 'class' of wares, upbringing and 'class' of the author, etc. This is of course part of the eternal problem with trying to quantify 'good taste/design' and one that could be said to be associated with the DIA Whilst the DIA did much for the promotion, status and elevation of the Poole Pottery, not to mention the rewarding number of commissions the pottery received, the rather negative, retrospective ideals and standards associated with the DIA did little for a highly commercial pottery looking to broaden it's customer base. The Poole Pottery exhibits and their presentation at the 1925 Paris Exhibition and the International Exhibition of Industrial Art in Leipzig two years later, show that Poole wares were not exactly revolutionary or particularly ground breaking when compared to many of the other exhibits of their Continental competition. One certainly could not label their wares 'modernist' in the strictest use of the term, in any way, in either shape or surface decoration. In fact, it was largely as a consequence of these two late 1920s exhibitions that any concessions to modernism began to appear in the Poole Pottery pattern books, even though, as is starting to be discovered through on-going research, many of these exotic and elaborate designs were 'borrowed' from Continental sources. Stella Beddoe of the Brighton Museum is gathering information related to some original sources for many Truda Adams designs, amongst others, which seem to owe a great deal to French textile and wallpaper designs, as well as other materials. Such designs, of course, would have been shunned by the likes of the DIA members, as being overtly decorative and bold.

The Carters could not have wished to find a more suitable exponent and practitioner of 'Art and Industry' issues than John Adams. Whilst Harold Stabler's official capacity at Poole was perhaps more on the sidelines, as external design consultant, making significant contributions in design and promotion, John Adams' involvement was to be far more practical. John Adams was given the title of Managing Director in the new partnership, although it was with his input into the area of design, especially shape design, along with his technical abilities, that he was to make his mark. He had developed his technical skills after working in Stoke-on-Trent in the tile industry and at Bernard Moore's pottery as a painter of lustre ware. He and his wife Truda later developed a pottery section with the School of Art in the Durban Technical College, South Africa, immediately before his arrival at Poole. One particular feature of John Adams' work which highlights the benefits of employing a designer was his ability to see and listen to what the demands of the buying public were, and then reflect those requirements in the shapes and designs he then produced. If the public wanted cigarette boxes, ashtrays, wall vases, jam pots, cheese dishes with covers, sandwich trays, etc, then that is what he designed.

Gertrude (Truda) Sharp, before she met and married John Adams, was a fellow student with John at the Royal College of Art. Her work for Poole was to be highly significant as the vast majority of the 1920s and 1930s surface pattern designs for the ornamental and decorative wares were designed by her, and if not by her then by

Early Carter, Stabler and Adams pottery designed by Truda Adams, J. Radley Young and Harold Stabler. Studio Yearbook, 1922.

her sister Minnie McLeish. Truda Adams (later married to Cyril Carter) is perhaps one of the most underestimated and overlooked female ceramic designers of the twentieth century, especially in light of the authorship concerning Susie Cooper, Clarice Cliff and Charlotte Rhead, and latterly on the designs of Jessie Tait for Midwinter and Susan Williams-Ellis for Portmeirion. Truda continued designing for Poole until her retirement in 1950 and even carried on as external consultant for a few more years.

Pheobe Stabler was a recognised sculptress, modeller and designer in her own right, exhibiting many works throughout the country in the major annual round of exhibitions related to the crafts and decorative arts. Her business acumen was revealed through the sale of several of her works, often with minor modifications or a change in title, to three or four different manufacturers, often for sale on the High Street, although in different media, at the same time.

The Stablers were able to bring to the new partnership some sculptures that they had modelled in previous years, some of which were hastily made at the Poole Works to be shown at the Feb/March 1921 British Industries Fair and then later in the year at the launch of the new partnership at Regent House, Kingsway in London. These figures and roundels were an important addition to the ornamental wares, and gave the display an extra interest and vital dimension which was picked up by many of the reviewers. The roundels would certainly have added colour and brightness, being decorated in the manner of the Italian 'Della Robbia' wares, to the display. The oval wall medallion 'Spring' and its companion 'Summer', the latter certainly displayed at Regent House (assuming the title to be correct), must have looked particularly stunning, with the brightly coloured Italianate colouring highlighting the heavily moulded basket of naturalistic flowers. By the following year the

pottery was able to put various other previously designed Stabler works into limited production, including the large and quite stunning model of The Bull, designed jointly by both Harold and Phoebe and in production until the 1903s, as well as the Picardy Peasants, the Buster Boy and the Lavender Woman, designed by Pheobe. New models included the two figures Bath Towel and Buster Girl designed by Pheobe Stabler. One of the most significant designs by Harold for the Poole Pottery was that of the Galleon, introduced in 1925, which became the unofficial symbol of the Pottery, being exhibited and illustrated constantly throughout the 1920s and 1930s. This in turn led to smaller, less colourful versions being designed later, some models with the name of the pottery on the base and used in shop advertising. At about the same time Harold also designed the highly Art Deco stylised models of The Goat and The Bear, both animals standing on very angular rocky outcrops.

In the first few years after the formation of the new partnership the output of the ornamental and decorative wares relied largely on what had been produced over the preceding few years,

Early Carter, Stabler and Adams pottery wares designed by Truda and John Adams. Studio Yearbook, 1922.

POOLE POTTERY EXECUTED BY CARTER STABLER AND ADAMS, POOLE, DORSET

Early Carter, Stabler and Adams pottery designed by Truda and John Adams and Ernest Bant(t)en. Studio Yearbook 1923.

namely the wares modelled and designed by James Radley Young, with the addition of the figurative works, mentioned above, by the Stablers. However, the Young wares began to be modified, as has previously been mentioned, by Truda Adams, bringing to them a new lease of life, developing from the 'simple, sound and practical . . .' and 'the ingenious juxtaposition of one or two simple colours . . .' (as reported in the Pottery and Glass Trades review in 1921) to the 'Distinctiveness of form, refined yet soft colour in free brushwork of painted patterns . . . pieces of stoneware enriched with blue, purple, and other rich colour schemes of fruits with greens of foliage, in underglaze treatment' reported two years later. It was not until about 1922 that the wares really began to change, a time which coincided with the introduction of a new red earthenware body, covered with a semi-matt grey tinted glaze and two years later the addition of a white slip together with the use of a clearer glaze with more technical alterations in the years to come. The surface pattern designs gradually began to become bolder and more confident throughout the early 1920s, with the flowers becoming more elaborate and much larger, taking up proportionally more of the surface of the vessel.

Between 1924 and 1927 the reputation of and interest in the new Poole Pottery was particularly strong, the wares being shown in many of the major International exhibitions of the period; including the British Empire Exhibition at Wembley (1924), the famous Paris Decorative and Industrial Arts Exhibition of 1925 (as a consequence of which we now have the term 'Art Deco') and the Leipzig International Exhibition of 1927. It was through the pottery's involvement with such exhibitions that John Adams, Harold Stabler and in particular Truda Adams would have seen and been influenced by the enormous variety of work that they saw on display there. Such influence was later to become apparent in the distinctive style that developed at Poole. There were also many slightly smaller exhibitions within Britain, such as that at those held in London at the Heal's Mansard Gallery, Bruton Place, and the Gieves Gallery, in Old Bond Street, along with the various British Industries Fairs. It would appear that during the important influential and formative early years of the new partnership, the wares produced at Poole were getting particular attention and publicity,

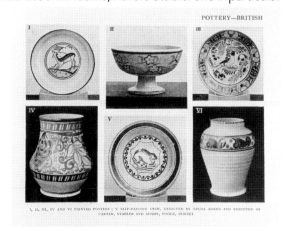

I, II, III, IV AND VI PAINTED POTTERY; V SLIP-PAINTED DISH, DESIGNED BY TRUDA ADAMS AND EXECUTED BY CARTER, STABLER AND ADAMS, POOLE, DORSET

Carter, Stabler and Adams wares designed by Truda Adams, the dish on the bottom centre decorated using coloured slip. Studio Yearbook, 1924.

certainly amongst the trade press, with favourable reviews accompanied more often than not by numerous illustrations with the text. The special exhibitions which were held in London to promote the new Poole Pottery wares also received generous coverage in the press. Compared to that devoted to other contemporary potteries such coverage was to say the least generous. Whether this has to do with a clever commercial and promotional strategy on behalf of the Carter, Stabler & Adams partnership or due to the influence, status or social connections of any of the partners, or was indeed based purely on the merits of the wares themselves, is open to question. Perhaps it was in part due to all three.

It was recognised at the time by certain critics that the employment and training of a new team of paintresses had done much to add to the development of the new lines. Initially this team consisted of paintresses who had worked under James Radley Young, namely Cissie Collett, Ann Hatchard and a Miss Kendall; these were joined by Margaret Holder and Ruth Pavely. The later two, particularly Ruth Pavely, were to make significant contributions to the Pottery. By the early 1930s there were over thirty paintresses working on what became known as the 'traditional' ware.

The introduction of bold colourful patterns, mostly based on stylised floral designs, repeated in bands, with the use of animals and birds as well, almost entirely covering the shape of the vessel, immediately caught the eye of the public and critics alike. It was the particularly striking use of bright and bold colours in such an enthusiastic manner that drew much praise. During the early 1920s there was an increased use of colour on many decorative art objects, especially those of France, which owed much to the bold use of colours seen in the theatre back drops and clothing used by the Russian Ballet, going back as early as 1909, as well in the contemporary paintings of the period. Society throughout Europe welcomed such as change, especially after the years of turmoil and struggle during the first World War. The plethora of exhibitions in Europe during the ten years after the war was arranged as much as to cajole industry and commerce into rapid development, as to tell the world and it's own citizens that Europe was back on its feet. For many the war was seen as a format to start with a clean slate, to change previously held ideas about buildings, housing, socially accepted norms, etc. It was seen as an opportunity for a shift in direction and ways of thinking. Each country, however, had its own responses to such notions, some more easily swayed, whilst others preferred a slower studied pace, picking at what it thought suitable for itself. Britain in the main was one of the latter.

In Britain new ideas concerning pattern, design and relationships between Art and Industry, often took some time to formulate and certainly to become accepted. The influence of what become known as Art Deco was very slow to catch on, but one of the first potteries to explore the possibilities of the new angular abstract style was Poole.

It was particularly the work of Truda Adams that brought this transition about. Her designs in the 1920s, especially for large vases, were truly magnificent with sixteen inch vases lavishly covered with bold bouquets and sprays of flowers, sometimes including birds, between banded, scalloped, chevron or wave bands. Truda designs ranged from the almost naturalistic, through very stylised to full-blown abstract and all during a very short period in the mid-1920s. Much of her work was inspired by French textile, carpet and fabric patterns, and as on-going research has revealed, Truda often drew heavily on designs by artists and designers such as E. A. Séguy, particularly some of his Egyptian inspired designs, as well as the work of René Buthaud. One could equally point to many other influences from the wrought-iron work and design of Edgar Brandt to printed packaging designs of the period. This is one of the many topics concerning the history of Poole, another being the Carter's & Co tile and architectural business, that has yet to be thoroughly explored and one that certainly needs further research.

Various influences can be identified both in relation to shape and surface decoration, and the influence of the 'Mediterranean' was certainly one. It should not be forgotten that this was time of the great discovery and learning, hastened by a fast growing and ever more efficient forms of communication. Egyptian tombs and civilisation, Aztec civilisation, Ancient Rome and Greece, to mention a few, figured large in the press, magazines, exhibitions and books of the period, as more and more discoveries were made from the beneath the earth and the sea. Just one example that directly relates to Poole designs is the interest generated by the works of the Della Robbia brothers, dating from the late 15th and early 16th centuries in Italy. Just before the turn of the Century, there were a number of major exhibitions of their bold and brightly coloured architectural works along with several new books about the life and work of the Della Robbia family. The Victoria and Albert Museum in London acquired numerous examples which then travelled the length of the country which in turn set off a whole stable of artists making works inspired by the wares. Harold and Pheobe Stabler are two shining examples in this mould, as we shall see. The use of such a bright palette may well have some bearing on the colouration of the surface pattern designs of Truda Adams, formerly a student of the RCA and therefore highly likely to have frequented the local Victoria and Albert Museum and also to have visited galleries and perhaps even artists, sculptors and designer's studios in Chelsea to see such works. Whatever the source of these designs on Poole Pottery they are now amongst the most sought after by collectors.

Additional inspiration was warmly welcomed and encouraged via the use of external artists, be they cartoonists, illustrators, sculptors or artists. This is something that has recurred throughout the history of the Poole Pottery to this day. Apart from the obvious diversity, fresh outlook and new approach that could be, and was, gleaned from such an influx, there is perhaps a deeper and more meaningful reason for the continued association, namely the relationship, often ambiguous as previously mentioned, between the artist and industry. This aspect of the Poole Pottery has often been overlooked but is as important today as it was in the early years. Harold Stabler was the great instigator of many external contacts with additional contacts being developed by Charles who persuaded graduates from the Royal College to provide some sketches either during or after a visit to the pottery, or perhaps even from just seeing examples of the ware. Erna Manners was one of the first to be involved for a short period, providing the 'Grape' and the 'Fuchsia' designs, the latter being the only Poole Pottery design to rightly use the name. Olive Bourne produced a series of designs based on female figures and heads in the late 1920s, with one dish of a female head appearing amongst the branches of a bush holding some food for a bird, which took pride of place in the centre of the Leipzig International Exhibition of Industrial Art in 1927. Harold Brownsword was a notable figure having trained in the Hanley school of art, later becoming the sculptor teacher for the Regent Street Polytechnic School of Art, London, 1914. At Poole, he modelled various items including bookends in the form of elephants, another pair as an equestrian figure, a commemorative plaque of King Edward VIII and a small ashtray with a figure. Hugh Llewellyn, the local headmaster of the Poole school of Art modelled a group of three monkeys, around 1922-23, which was then later released as a slip cast figure using a stoneware body. Various other artists also contributed to the tile production side, as will be seen in a later chapter.

In another interesting departure from what was considered 'normal practice' in the home of the Potteries, Stoke-on-Trent, paintresses were often allowed to submit designs of their own which could be and often were put into production, several lasting many years. Such a practice in the Potteries was, if it ever took place, never admitted in public, the head designer always being given the credit, as was the case with one or two Moorcroft designs during the transition from father to son, and also in several cases at the Wilkinson/Newport works under the head designer Clarice Cliff. In the latter case, the reasons were more to do with keeping the gravy train of publicity and promotion on track than anything else, especially as the factory was to continue to make the most of the designer's name on their trade mark in the decades after Clarice had ceased serious involvement in the pottery.

As Truda Adams' confidence grew into the 1920s, along with a heightened demand from the public and a growing acceptance of European-style highly stylised and abstract designs, so she began to reflect the Continental flavour. By 1926-7 minimalist floral patterns began to appear, still in bold colours, along with highly exotic all over patterns in semi-abstract floral and foliate motifs. Truda also began experimenting with the colour palette into the 1930s, sometimes using just two colours against the pale white slip, or just three or four colours. Occasionally Truda even altered the colour of the slip to a pale pink or pastel grey. By the 1934, a white earthenware body was introduced, altering the look and feel of the wares. Gone was the soft and gentle warmth of the red bodied wares and in came a sharper, brighter and cleaner look. The patterns, previously slightly subtle and subdued, become crisp and more defined, many looking to the angularity of European works and some distinctly highly abstract, almost mechanical in the use of toothed wheels or gears, washers and bearings as motifs.

The use of such abstract patterns on pottery was seen very much as a short-term fashion statement and was marketed as such by several potteries. The peak of perfection of this style can be seen in the designs by Eric Slater for Shelley, most notably in the minimalist surface patterns that adorned so well the new angular shapes of 'Vogue ' and 'Mode' that he designed. Looking at some of the highly abstract patterns and motifs on Poole one sometimes has to wonder about the marriage with some of the shapes. But one doesn't have to look far for the answer with the introduction of the wonderfully abstract shapes designed by John Adams between 1930 and 1933, 'Everest' and 'Plane'. However, the only decoration that was used on these shapes was a minimalist use of coloured bands, as befits such wonderfully geometric shapes.

As previously indicated, such fashionable wares were made in relatively limited numbers when compared to the high volume mass-production which a commercial factory required to survive. These 'high-end' wares were seen very much as the flagship of the pottery and were used as such to generate and promote interest. Once in the public eye the ordinary more affordable volume wares could be brought in for those wishing to be seen to be in fashion and vogue.

For today's collectors the most sought after pieces are these 'high-end' pieces, the extremes of which are the pieces made specifically for exhibitions, that generate the most interest and highest prices. Other collectable items during this period include the John Adams designed candlesticks of grape-laden vine, in a particularly French manner, and those with pierced or solid birds in flight amongst branches or birds perched in branches. These were made in various sizes and designed to hold single or multiple candles. Numerous examples of the experimental wares developed by John Adams can also be found, many with glaze effects inspired by the contemporary interest in Studio Pottery, initiated by Bernard Leech, as well as various examples with Oriental-inspired glazes.

For most of us, we have become familiar with the wares of Poole Pottery through the use, handling, collecting and/or selling of the high volume mass-produced ordinary everyday functional and ornamental wares. Items such as jam pots and covers, biscuit barrels and covers (with cane handles), cheese dishes and covers, posy bowls, candlesticks, egg cups, ashtrays, jugs and beakers. These wares, in many respects, are the important wares of the Poole Pottery as it is due to the sale of these wares that the company managed to survive. Although the glory and adulation went to the few highly decorative and expensive to produce wares, the pottery's continued existence would not have been possible without the volume sales of the domestic ware ranges. Amongst the ordinary wares there are some wonderful shape and surface pattern designs, many adapted from the larger pieces, such as the Harold Brownsword and John Adams bee box and cover, various hors d'oeuvres trays and powder bowls and covers.

One of the most important and significant additions to the domestic wares offered by Poole was the revolutionary 'Streamline' shape designed by John Adams in 1935-36. Ernest Baggaley developed the finishing touch by creating a new Vellum semi-matt glaze which could be produced in a range of new colours. A combination of two of the colours was chosen for the new range. The interior of the teapots, coffee pots and hot water pots were usually white. What was particularly important about the new glaze was that it was fairly viscous and very durable and impervious to water, significant attributes for a heavily-used tableware service, but the most important was that the glaze was highly consistent. The result was that Poole now had a standardised tableware service, achieved with the new shape and combination glaze effects. This meant that very high volume turnover could be achieved in terms of production, feeding the hungry Dressler tunnel ovens, but also that importantly, the losses, or defective wares, were dramatically reduced as a consequence of the standardisation. The fact that the decoration did not involve any expensive and time consuming hand-painting and that the shapes could be made mechanically or semi-mechanically using mass production methods, significantly reduced costs. It is perhaps interesting that one year later, in 1937, a third Dressler tunnel oven was installed in the White Works reflecting not only the need to fire an even greater number of wares but also that Poole had some very healthy order books to be able to afford to install yet another such kiln. What it meant to the Poole Pottery was that they could produce a high volume of ware for a minimal cost and therefore create new markets as well as developing old ones.

The development of the Streamline range was a huge shift in direction for Poole Pottery, thanks largely to the efforts of John Adams and the ingenious introduction by him to the firm of Ernest Baggaley from Stoke on Trent. The new glaze effects helped bring about the development of new shapes including Everest, which was developed in 1931 and launched in the following year, followed by Plane ware and Picotee, the latter involving some forty-three banded glazing permutations at least. It was as if a new lease of life had entered the pottery with the introduction of flying bird ornaments, shells, wall vases, models of sailing ships and other items, all making use of the simplicity of the two-tone glaze effects or the glazes used on the Picotee wares. These wares were made and even targeted at the lower end of the buying market, thereby broadening the pottery's customer base. The change in public buying demands, due to alterations in society, such as the building of smaller houses, the increased use of electrical domestic products and other behavioural patterns often related to class, was something that John Adams had been aware of and was now able to address.

It was thanks to the development of the Streamline range and all that it meant in terms of standardisation, that Poole Pottery could look forward to a highly successful commercial future.

The Tile Business
1918-39

All that had been built up and put in place before 1914 at Carter & Co had to be put on hold during the war, although, as previously mentioned, some developments in tile production were made with the introduction of tin-glazed tile production. Even more significant was the introduction of single pictorial tile designs by Joseph Roelants. In addition to this the numerous brightly coloured and expressionistic tile designs by Roger Fry and others of the Bloomsbury group, not to mention their table ware and ornamental pottery, would not have gone unnoticed at the pottery.

The post-war period offered little immediate promise for decorative tiling with a shift towards plain monochrome coloured machine made tiles. As far as Carter & Co were concerned from a commercial level this was fine as they were ready to cope with such high volume demand through the Dressler tunnel oven, even though the oven could be difficult at times. Other tileries were not so well prepared.

More importantly Carter & Co were now, as one of the country's leading firms, almost expected to lead rather than follow. This was part of the great transition that the firm underwent during the post-war period and into the 1920s. The transformation was brought about as a result of many factors but the pictorial tiles of Roelants and the artistic influence of the Bloomsbury Group certainly opened the eyes and minds of those at Carters to the potential and possibilities of what could be achieved. The frequent praise and mentions directed at the exhibited Dutch inspired tiles by Roelants between 1917 and 1920 would not have gone unnoticed.

The Blue Dutch and Coloured Dutch series designed by Joseph Roelants, are some of the earliest tin-glazed tiles made at Carters, possibly as early as 1917. There are twelve designs known in this series and they were produced in blue or in coloured versions executed by hand painting. The Dutch series were the first in a new line of picture tiles utilising the tin-glazed technique produced at the new look Carter, Stabler & Adams, established in 1921 following the death of Owen Carter, and may well pre-date this new partnership. In 1917 Carter & Co had a medium sized stand (number L6) at the British Industries Fair, held in the Victoria & Albert Museum, opposite the stand of J Sadler, (makers of teapots and related wares) Stoke on Trent. In the 1917 Board of Trade exhibition catalogue under the lengthy list of the types of tiles and related architectural fittings that Carter could supply is listed "Hand painted Anglo-Dutch Glazed Tiles…" which would seem to indicate that the Roelants' designs were available at this time. The same two series were later produced using newly developed silk-screen printed techniques in the 1950s and 1960s.

It is interesting to note, as pointed out by Chris Blanchett (editor of 'Glazed Expressions', the quarterly magazine of the Tile and Architectural Ceramic Society) that the blue screen printed designs used three shades of blue to give the appearance of the earlier hand painted tiles, while the coloured versions used up to seven screens. It would appear that the screen printed versions were almost as time consuming as the earlier hand painted versions, the major difference being the de-skilling effect, and consequent reduced labour cost, of the screened tile.

Returning to the earlier period far rarer is the hand painted Blue Boats series, another of Roelants' designs, probably dating from the same period, as well as the Coloured Boat series. As with the previous Dutch series, these were also later to be produced by the silk-screen method. The injection of new artistic and technical skills with the arrival of the Stablers and the Adams's introduced a sudden shift in emphasis with the introduction of numerous freelance designers and artists, as well as in the resident designers producing designs for tiles. The results of the continual fresh input of new innovative tile designs made Carter & Co one of the most influential tile firms in the 1920s.

With the arrival of Harold and Phoebe Stabler at Carter & Co, the faience department executed many new commissions. The first such commission was the massive War Memorial for Durban, South Africa, completed in 1925, depicting two larger than life angels holding the body of Christ between them, a radiating sun behind with a dove above, all in bright Della Robbia style colours. This was by far the largest and most important architectural commission executed by the Poole Pottery. Other large works designed by the Stablers, and again in Della Robbia-style colouring, included the Rugby School War Memorial, executed before the Durban memorial in 1922 and the religious faience panels exhibited at the 1924 British Empire exhibition, later installed in the Mary Abbot's Kensington Infirmary mortuary chapel and recently dismantled and installed back at the Poole Pottery.

During the 1920s there was a massive and long awaited house building programme throughout Britain. Even before 1914 there had been a serious shortage of new houses, the First World War only exacerbated the problem. Between 1919 and 1939 four million new houses were built in England and Wales; the vast majority of those in the 1920s. Added to this electricity for use in homes which had been available since the 1890s became cheap enough to be affordable by those with very moderate incomes, with virtually all the new houses being wired for electricity. On the strength of this, numerous electrical household appliances were developed and sold, including cookers, heaters, lighting, water heating, etc, all promoted as necessary for the efficient and hygienic running of a household. All new houses built after 1919 had to have a bathroom installed, less than 10 per cent of households having them before.

An Alfred Read designed vase used in a promotional display for Fragonard Ltd Irish linen. Design magazine, 1957.

Another important interior feature of the new house building was the fireplace. This industry or subsidiary industry was to see a rapid growth in the number of businesses devoted to the supplying and fitting of fireplaces during the 1920s and continuing though to the 1980s. Various associations of fireplace manufacturers were set up to help establish industry standards, for joint promotion of all members and their interests. National Fireplace Association still going in 1995, with members being part of the National Fireplace Manufacturers Association. There was also the British Ceramic Tile Council, the Glazed & Floor Tile Home Association and the Glazed & Floor Tile Export Association all of which had prior to 1960 been called The Glazed & Floor Tile Manufacturers' Association.

As a consequence of the new building programme, along with the emphasis on hygiene, not only in public housing but numerous other buildings such as hospitals, hotels and public lavatories, there was an extraordinary demand for tiles. Tiles were seen as being easy to clean and therefore hygienic as well as durable. Such was the emphasis on the sterility of tiles that whole rooms were often tiled, floors, walls and even the ceiling. Hospitals were one of the main users of such tiles. Throughout much of the twentieth century whilst corridors, wards, operating rooms, etc, in hospitals have been tiled with monochrome or simple repeated tiling, there has been a special demand for more pictorial tiles in children's wards. Up and down the country, there is still today plenty of evidence of some wonderful tile panels and series of individual tiles in situ in many hospitals. Thanks to John Greene, a member of the Tile and Architectural Society (TACS), there is now a far greater public awareness and even a conservation campaign devoted to the protection of the numerous tiles schemes still in hospitals. This has been underlined with the publication of his book, *Brightening the Long Days. Hospital Tile Pictures* which was published by the TACS. The designs used in many of the schemes were carried out by Carter & Co, designed by Harold Stabler, Dora M Batty, Joseph Roelants, James Radley Young, E. E. Strickland and Phyllis Butler. The tile schemes ranged from the use of previously designed individual series, sometimes used on four tiles as a variation, to large multiple tile panels of anything up to nine feet. Many of the tile schemes were illustrated in a promotional booklet dating from about 1935; *Carter Picture Tiles for Hospitals*. There were occasionally larger panels executed but nothing could possibly have been larger than the 'All the Fun of the Fair', installed at the Middlesex Hospital, London, a twenty-six foot by seven foot and six inch panel that covered an entire wall of the Bernard Baron Ward, the design in this case being by Hadyn Jensen in 1929.

The various Dutch tiles series by Joseph Roelants, mentioned above, are typical of the sort of tiling found in some of the hospitals along with other more specific designs related to children, many of which were inspired by children's books illustrated by designers such as Mabel Lucie Attwell. Tile series such as Nursery Rhymes and Nursery Toys were a particular favourite designed by Dora Batty, a graduate of the Royal College, during the early 1920s. Another series, Playbox was designed by A. B. Read although probably slightly later into the 1930s. These were also later to be produced using screen prints in the 1950s and later.

One series of tile designs, Waterbirds, by Harold Stabler, dating to between 1921-25, can be found in nurseries and on Nursery tablewares, and was still being produced on tiles in the 1950s. Harold was responsible for persuading Edward Bawden, another Royal College student, to produce some designs for tiles, entitled The Chase and Sporting, designed in about 1922. Both of these series were hand painted and could still be ordered in to the 1950s, although the later editions were very different. Bawden also made a significant contribution to the typographic

Poole pottery in a South African retailers store on new demountable display stands designed by Robert Wetmore. Design magazine 1957.

Poole Pottery house style, designing numerous wood cut illustrations which were used as part of various advertising and promotional literature. A booklet published in 1922 entitled 'Pottery Making at Poole' was wonderfully illustrated by Bawden with amusing scenes showing some of the processes involved in the making of Poole pottery. The frontispiece of this book depicting a map of Poole with the pottery, High Street, railway station and other local landmarks, was converted into two tile panels by Margaret Holder in 1930. One panel was located on the staircase leading to the old showroom and another, with the addition of a bus station and a bus, was situated in the Bournemouth bus station. The former panel can now be seen in the present Poole Pottery museum while the latter seems to have disappeared. Some details of these designs along with others designed by Bawden were used to decorate the visitor's tea room which opened in 1932.

One of the most commonly seen and well known of these early pictorial tiles is the Farmyard series, designed by E. E. Strickland in about 1922, in both single tile and four-tile panels. It is the latter four-tile panels seen in Dewhurst butcher's shops and Mac Fisheries all around Britain that are perhaps the best known. The technique on these tiles was slightly unusual in that after the blocks of colour had been applied using stencils, a hand painted black outline was used to cover up any white gaps or over laps that might have occurred in the first process, also to add details and highlights. In the post-war period the colours used became very harsh and lacked the softness of line. Three more stencilled tile designs were developed as a consequence of Farmyard, namely; Seagull possibly by Irene Fawkes, Caller Herrin' by Dora M Batty and Fishing Smacks by Minnie McLeish, all designed between 1921 and 1925 and made for Mac Fisheries. These designs along with four others were also made to be used on pot lids.

In order to be ahead of the field Owen Carter and Harold Stabler realised the need to invest in youth with a knowledge of what might be required in contemporary settings. With this is mind they took on another graduate of the Royal College of art, Reginald Till, in 1923, at the tile works. Till was responsible for introducing new methods of surface decoration as well as re-introducing old methods but employing them in a different manner. Tube-lining was one such technique, and was adapted for single and panel tile production during the late 1920s and 1930s. More usually associated with the swirling free-flowing designs of Art Nouveau at the turn of the century, Reginald Till used the raised lines created by trailing liquid clay onto the surface of a tile not only to separate colours, creating blocks or areas of solid colour (much as in stencilling or later silk screen printing) but also as part of the pattern. Tube-lining was effectively used on large multi-tile panels, for introducing lettering and for special effects, such as the panel for the Building Trades Exhibition of 1930. If there was a complex repeated geometric design on a single tile, this was usually more economically produced by moulded-raised lines or press-lined tiles. Just before Reginald Till retired, in 1951-52, he was responsible for the development of yet another new and very important innovative decorative tile technique, namely silk-screen printing.

During this period, there were various floral tile series, two produced by Reginald Till and others by Truda Carter. Flowers designed by Truda Carter and Reginald Till, Truda Carter adapting her colourful designs from her tablewares for tiles. Freelance artists were used frequently at Carters as has already been seen, and the dog tile designs by Cecil Aldin, six in all, dating from the 1930s are typical examples. The fact that the designs appear with the artist's facsimile signature whereas other artist's work such as Bawden's did not, relates to more to a compositional effect than anything else.

As we have already seen in a previous chapter, Poole were not adverse to supplying smaller concerns with blank tiles which would then be decorated and returned to the pottery to be fired, should the customer require it. William De Morgan along with Roger Fry and a few fellow members of the Bloomsbury Group were artists who took advantage of this facility. In 1929 and into the 1930s Sylvia Packard and Rosalind Ord initially relied on Carters to supply them with tiles during the fledging years of their tile decorating concern which soon became a full-scale business and is now trading as Marlborough Ceramic Tiles, in Wiltshire. Many of the early Packard and Ord tiles, usually marked with a combined 'OR' on the front, often appeared to be influenced by (sometimes were even confused with) Carters tile designs, perhaps due to the method of decoration and choice of subject matter. It was not long, however, before the company of Packard and Ord had established their own fluent house style and even started to compete with Carters.

This peripheral influence, although somewhat loose, even extended to tiles produced in South Africa at Olisfantsfontein. John and Truda Adams having established a ceramics curriculum in the Durban School of Art between 1915 and 1921, had a great influence on Gladys Short, Marjorie Johnstone and Joan Methley, students of the school of art, who came together to produce architectural ceramics. Later joined by Audrey Frank and Thelma Currie this group produced wares in much the same vein as Carters, using Della Robbia glazes and roundels, as well as tin-glazed tiles decorated with in-glaze designs. Some of the pattern designs often bear a striking similarity to the work of Dora Batty and the Adams's. Other miscellaneous tile sets were designed by numerous resident and visiting artists, and all too often the resident designers designs were unattributed or gained little recognition. The work of Arthur Nickols is a case in point. Nickols specialised in the execution of the larger painted panel scenes, such as rural landscapes, scenes with cattle or sheep for butchers or various fishing scenes for fish shops, often designed by J R Young, whose name appears along the base of the panel but not that of Nickols. Nickols is recorded as having designed one set of wall tiles, Dairy, dating from the 1920s and Fish in the 1930s but almost certainly designed more. Certainly, one of his most impressive designs of a dolphin leaping over bottle kiln was recognised as such, becoming one of the symbols, along with the majestic galleon designed by Harold Stabler, of the Poole Pottery. It would also appear that the tube-lined Alphabet tile set of the 1930s might also be his work, given that Nickols used the technique to such a large extent in his large panels for town maps, although this could equally have been designed by Reginald Till. Again it was either Till or Nickols who was responsible for the design of the Poole Swimming Club stoneware plaque, dating from 1932, which has a tube-lined leaping dolphin much in the same vein as an earlier design by Nickols. Many of the tiled signs for public houses and other buildings made during this period also seem likely to be the work of Nickols.

Some of the biggest, most prestigious and time consuming achievements for the Carter & Co concern the work carried out for some of the new modern and innovatory buildings of the period, the most significant being the Firestone Factory in Brentford, Middlesex, the massive Hoover factory, Perivale and the De La Warr Pavilion, at Bexhill-on-Sea in Sussex. Both the Firestone and Hoover buildings were striking in terms of visual appearance through the combination of the design and the use of Carters tiling to achieve the colours and visual effect desired by the architects. The De La Warr Pavilion was a very different achievement in terms of complex decorative faience work as opposed to the simple coloured tiling of the buildings above.

One of Carter's commissions, which owes much to the social connections of Harold Stabler and Cyril Carter, was the work carried out for the London Underground. Harold designed some eighteen individual relief moulded tiles, between 1938-39, depicting well known buildings; including St Paul's and the House's of Parliament, as well as motifs such as the circle and line design of the London Underground. These were placed in decorative schemes mainly on the City Line. The success and demand for tiles and architectural faience during the 1930s brought with it many problems mostly related to factory space and firing capacity. The firing capacity had already been improved in 1927 with the introduction of a Williamson continuous firing tunnel oven installed at the Architectural Pottery works and a second Dressler tunnel oven built at the White Works. The problems of space were solved, as they had always been, by continually adding buildings onto already existing ones in a very sporadic fashion. In 1937, with demand for wall and floor tiles ever increasing, a third Dressler tunnel oven was installed in the White Works, the building having to be extended in the process.

In many respects it seems a little odd that during the 1930s the designers at Carters did not create some highly stylish and then very fashionable geometric high Art Deco and abstract tile designs of the type being executed by Maws, of Jackfield, Shropshire, Pilkington's of Manchester, Candy & Co and one or two other firms. On reflection, this may well be due to the business philosophy of sticking with the tried, tested and successful, namely the softer and appealing pictorial subjects unless of course the readers know of any geometric Art Deco tiling? This attitude was, however, to change dramatically in the post-war period following the arrival of a new group of designers and managers. Oddities do and will continue to appear, which is all part of the fun of collecting. In 1995 a rare tube-lined four tile panel clock face, dating from about 1935, was discovered, the numbers appearing against variously coloured balloon images, with a clown standing in the middle, wearing a red peaked hat and a star studded yellow-ground costume. The clown had no arms, as these would have been made out of metal to form the hands of the clock. As the clock was not pierced in the centre for the spindle to protrude through to rotate the arms, I think it is safe to assume that this particular set of tiles never full-filled their ultimate task.

There were of course numerous tiles, sets of tiles and panels made during this period and the ones mentioned above are perhaps some of the better known ones. The large number of hotel and public house contracts, including those for Carrington's, Mann, Courage's, Watney Combe, together with those for banks, cinemas, private houses and shipping that were undertaken by Carters would provide enough information to fill the pages of a book in themselves. Numerous miles of tiling were sent abroad to cover the floor of the Jamaica Cathedral, with other tiles finding their way to Shanghai, Vladivostock and Chile. The public schools of Haileybury, Winchester and Cranford have Carter's tiles as do some other well known companies, including Frys, Cadbury's, Schweppes, Shell House, the headquarters of the BBC and even the Bank of England. It was because of such plentiful national contracts that Carters remained one of the largest tile firms. There would appear to be a great deal of research to be done in this field, with plenty of archival material largely unruffled for many years in the Poole Pottery.

In 1928, Carter & Co Ltd became a public company, being joined by Carter & Co (London) Ltd, Carter, Stabler and Adams Ltd and the Art Pavements and Decorations Ltd. Further additions followed in 1931 and 1932 with J. H. Barrett & Co Ltd and the Marbolith Flooring Co. Ltd, respectively, being purchased. The introduction of spray glazing and the re-development of tube-lining are two of the many contributions made by Reginald Till during his highly important and productive years working at Carters but those years were to end with the introduction of yet another significant and arguably even more important decorative process; silk-screen printing. Another of the many innovative ideas that kept Carter & Co at the leading edge of the tile and architectural business.

Post War Style & Design
1945 to 1960s

The years of the Second World War saw the virtual shut-down of the Poole pottery, with the work force reduced to a handful, most of the buildings being used for storage or offices and Cyril Carter taking part in a counter-espionage group involved with interviewing immigrants. With only a small export market, Carters' could not justify staying open to fulfil orders and develop others. Other potteries, mostly involved with bone china, were able to continue with overseas trade thereby securing valuable revenue for the war effort. At Poole some wares were made, as there was still a demand for functional everyday items for the numerous war-time brides, replacements for ware damaged or lost through bombing, as well as for military use and as a result of evacuations.

There were various reasons for the imposition of undecorated monochrome ware to be sold on the home market, minimum staff requirement, minimum resources, quicker production, etc, but Government policy had much to do with the extreme restrictions of such ware. The government, or rather the Board of Trade, in turn listened to the various 'Advisory Committees' that were set up with various specialist members on specific related committees. Largely through the efforts of eminent modernist design stalwarts such as Gordon Russell, John Cloag, Enid Marx, A .B Read and others, the Government was persuaded to enforce a strict policy of no or minimum decoration, monochrome colour, if colour had to be used at all and standardisation, amongst other things. The new 'Utility' ethos was promoted in exhibitions put on by the Board of Trade, such as the one in October 1942, as well as being advertised widely in magazines and through articles in the press, all in an attempt to gain public acceptance. The latter was not forthcoming, nor were the manufacturers at all pleased by what they saw as Government interference, but during the war years they accepted their lot. The hoped for emergence in the immediate post-war years, of a new simpler and more modernist approach to general industrial design throughout industry, as had been advocated from the 'form follows function' edicts of the 'Advisory' groups, did not occur. The quashing of decoration and colour during the war only made the thirst for pattern and colour all the more desirable for the British public and in turn the manufacturers.

At Poole, the answer to Utility was simple enough as the Streamline range, designed by John Adams in 1935-36, more than fitted the guidelines. The two colour glazes that had been used before the war were reduced

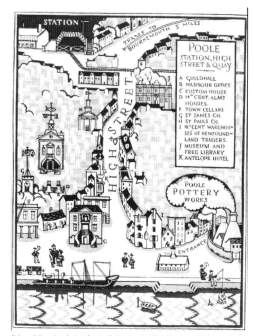

Edward Bawden design for Poole Pottery booklet, 'Pottery Making at Poole', published by the Curwen press in 1922. In about 1930 the same design was made into a tile panel, which can now be seen in the museum.

to a single white crystal glaze, and Ernest Baggaley remodelled some of the shapes, most noticeably the replacement of the slim finial with a button mushroom finial.

With the restrictions and shortages of industrial wares, a percentage of the public turned to studio pottery, exempt from industrial restrictions, with its coloured glazes, incised, faceted and cut decoration, as a way of adding colour and interest to the table.

During and after the War there was a new lease of life and popularity surrounding the crafts in general but specifically the work of the studio potters. Numerous small potteries even sprang up in response to the demand in the late 1940s, with men returning from the war and moving into less demanding types of work than they had had before the war and as a complete change from the strictures imposed by the services. The Rye pottery established by the Cole brothers, the Crowan Pottery established by Harry and May Davis and the Briglin Pottery, although producing very different types of ware, burst onto the market place with orders constantly flowing in. The restrictions imposed on the commercial pottery industry were to remain until 1952, allowing such new and old rural and/or studio potteries to gain from the demand, their wares often being sold in high street shops such as Woolworth's. Large London retail stores, such as Heal's and Peter Jones, during this period needed to fill their shelves with pottery to supply the growing demand for such wares in anything but white. Lucie Rie, at one time supplying buttons to the fashion industry, later had her own 'urban' ceramic wares exhibited at the Henry Rothschild Primavera Gallery, as did Bernard Leach and Katherine Pleydell-Bouverie.

The cry for colour was a constant theme amongst magazines and journals of the period. In the 1951/52 Daily Mail Ideal Home book it stated that "Apart from a few rare export rejects, all the pottery supplied to the shops comes from individual artists, or 'studio potters', as they are called in the trade. Our Great Midland Potteries are entirely given over to export trade, and the studio potters are responding well to the opportunity this situation opens up for them. Sighing a little inevitably, but brave, they are abandoning their beloved pots, beautiful but largely useless, and making instead fine sturdy cups, saucers and jugs for our breakfast tables and our nurseries." Although somewhat trite in tone the author continues. "Trends in pottery are following, in the most interesting way, the general longing for colour. Just as our walls have escaped from the exhaustive perpetual white and cream, our tables demand clear bright pieces for us to eat and drink from. The work of the Briglin Potteries and Brannam ware is especially charming from this point of view. The work of most of our best British potters can be recognised as easily as a Toulouse Lautrec or a Graham Sutherland painting. There is a Mrs. Lucie Rie, thought by some to be the best potter in London." The author of this statement obviously does not realise that Mrs. Rie is in fact an émigré and therefore not a typically British potter, in the true sense. More importantly, however, the work of Lucie Rie as well as other émigrés in Britain did bring a fresh approach and outlook to the British ceramic scene that was to be taken up and developed by others.

FOXTON FABRICS, POOLE POTTERY, LYGON STOOLS, DRYAD CANE & METAL WORK, ROWLEY WOOD PICTURES. These, and many other excellent things for Christmas Gifts for those who appreciate fine craftsmanship, at

EDWARD HARLAND & SONS
North Parade, Bradford.

This advertisement, designed by Frank Gayton, speaks for itself in the way it harmonises the lettering with the illustration. It is dignified, says little, but suggests much to the public.

Edward Harland & Sons, North Parade, Bradford. Dated 1923, this retailers advert was used in a discussion on the merits of promoting good design through the use of advertising in the Pottery Gazette trade magazine. It features an early James Young unglazed Carters vase, although it is interesting to see that the vase was referred to as 'Poole Pottery'. Of further interest is the surrounding contemporary furniture and decorative wares.

It was, of course, hoped, at least amongst the Gordon Russell fraternity, that this new demand for studio pottery might lead to them having some say in future industrial production. However, just by looking at the type and styles of ware being made during this pre-1952 period, it could be seen that much of the ware was customer generated. The new potteries were often making brightly coloured wares or wares that would sell quickly, even the formerly well established firms, seeing the prevailing fashions and demand, altered their normal studio practices to make more saleable wares.

What has the interest in studio pottery to do with the commercial wares of Poole Pottery? Well, initially not a great deal but the interest studio pottery generated in the public, whether it was one of disgust or pleasure, stayed and was to have a significant resurgence in the 1970s, this time within the commercial industry. Any immediate effect, in terms of commercial pottery and the lifting of restrictions in May 1952, was if anything to generate a longing for the exotic, lavishly shaped and colourfully decorated wares that the public had been used to before the war rather than the imposition of 'Utility' wares. It must be said that there is a growing opinion amongst some of today's authors of design history, that the 'traditional' or typically decorated floral patterned wares with gilt edging, so despised by the 'educated' critics (often middle class) and purveyors of taste at the time, have their merits and place amongst representative nationalistic designs. Such wares with representational floral patterns and often overly complex shapes are seen as quintessentially English, or as part of 'British tradition' and 'heritage', differentiating the British from its European neighbours.

Even though much of European and British design had been curtailed by the war, other countries carried on or were quick to regenerate after the war and it is here, between the late 1930s and to the late 1940s, that the foundations were laid for the explosive surge in design in the early 1950s. A radical transformation of not only the shape and surface decoration of objects and forms but also in many cases the materials used in their construction. On a further level the ideology and psychology of the pre-war years had changed with the broadening of nationalistic concerns onto a more International platform or forum. American aid fuelled the rebuilding of Italian homes and industry, European émigrés in Britain and America gave new direction and impetus to various areas and aspects of design, at the same time creating a network of communication channels with former colleagues and associates now widely scattered. Exhibitions proved to be a highly constructive way of bringing all of these Internationalist elements together, helping to enforce the cross fertilisation of ideas, renew and develop associations amongst the design fraternity and educate the public at the same time. As an example of the helping hand across the oceans, the House of Italian Handicrafts was opened in New York in 1947, through which Italian craftsworkers and American retailers could meet, all thanks to the Handicraft Development Incorporated in America.

What particularly marked out Italian design, post 1946, for special interest was the large amount of trial and experimentation that was allowed in small and medium sized firms, many based in and around Milan. Whilst some of these experiments can be said to have gone to extremes, it was through the persistence of such a huge variety and wealth of work that styles and future sources of influence were born. Typical of the innovative work of this early period are designs for furniture by Carlo Mollino and Franco Albini, whilst Marcelo Fantoni and Antonia Campi made wildly exuberant and boldly colourful ceramics, unfettered by any previous styles. What in fact became 'Italian style'.

Whilst exhibitions such as the 'Organic Design in Home Furnishings', held at the Museums of Modern Art. New York in 1940 might be said by some to have influenced the emergence of the new 'soft forms', such inspiration can be seen as coming from the work of the Surrealist sculptors and painters some twenty years earlier. Even more markedly, the use of rounded organic styling, in the field of decorative arts, can be seen in the work of designers from Sweden, Finland and Denmark. Specifically one could mention the works of Wilhelm Kage for Gustavsberg, Sweden, from the late 1930s, ceramic tablewares and ornamental wares by Kaj Frank for the Arabia pottery, in Finland, Alvar Aalto's and Aino Aalto's revolutionary design for glass and wood as well as Hans Wenger and Arne Jacobsen to name a few. The Scandinavian countries along with the Dutch had a greater interest in their work being more in tune with and sympathetic with the materials, whilst still being highly sculptural and innovative. Instead of taking things to the extremes, as the Italians often did, these designers were more concerned with utilising the qualities within the materials, with the materials, especially new ones such as plywood, often dictating the form.

Many of these new developments and ideas were to have a marked effect at the Poole Pottery, not only in terms of the visual appearance and styling of wares but also into the attitudes and awareness of the management as to the need to make the most of such market forces. This resulted, as we shall see, in the inauguration of the Poole Studio, established along lines seen in Scandinavian potteries.

There were many other designers involved in the post-war rejuvenation and many more influences, such as American Abstract Art, French fashion, etc, all of which were to play a part in the fast-emerging 'New Look' as it was to become known. More than anything else, however, this new style was fuelled by a sudden change in the consumer market with a rapid growth in demand from high income earning young adults or young newly weds. Along with the new consumer came new life style expectations and demands which were developed from a desire to move away from anything associated with the previous generation. Just as the Italians admired the American lifestyle, although mostly gleaned from Hollywood imagery, so the new young Americans came to love the Italian chic and debonair style, initially promoted through the early trade links and then celebrated and glorified in the numerous Hollywood movies. This was also an influence on many in Britain where a passion for a new life style was equally strong amongst the younger generation. Typical symbols such as the coffee houses, the Vespa scooter and pointed shoes, along with the music, much of it developed in Britain, signify the cross fertilisation of this new style.

Pottery played a relatively minor role compared to the impact of furniture, fabrics and the new industrial design products but it still had a significant contribution as part of the 'New Look' of the period. There were, however, certain criteria and expectations associated with the new ceramic wares. Bone china had for many of the young consumers associations with the past and connotations of a certain lifestyle to be avoided. New shapes were called for, more in tune with the changing living and life styles. Different and more affordable ways of buying tea, dinner and everyday wares saw the introduction of boxed starter or part sets, ideal for wedding presents or for buying when funds allowed. In Britain, after the sudden rise in television sales following the Coronation of Elizabeth II in 1953, the 'television sandwich set' was born. Vases and plant pots become extremely popular with the associated growth of floral and/or arrangements of twigs that become part of the 'New Look'.

These new developments were soon to form a highly significant part of the Poole pottery output, in fact Poole was to become one of the most innovative and highly regarded potteries over the next two decades and more. It must be remembered that whilst all of the above was taking place, largely between 1944 and the early 1950s, war restrictions on the whole of the commercial British Pottery industry meant that nothing could be made for the home market and very little for the export market until 1952. It must have been enormously frustrating to have been a designer in any field in Britain during this period, with restrictions, limited supplies of materials and a generally underdeveloped largely pre-war mechanised industry, watching and reading about what was going on in Italy, Scandinavia, America and to an extent, in terms of fashion, in France.

However, certain industries did manage to make an impression during these early years these were ones in which the designer could get involved, namely the fabric and wallpaper industries. Initially American led area of the late 1940s, where the textile and wallpaper industries had a close relationship, the British took on board the modern styles then pushed them even further until in 1951 Lucienne Day won the Gold Medal at the Milan Triennale for her 'Calyx' design, commissioned by Heal's. Leading Internationally known artists such as Henri Matisse, Eduardo Paolozzi, Henry Moore, Barbara Hepworth, Graham Sutherland and Alexander Calder, amongst others, were to design patterns for silk scarves created by the silk-screen process. As a consequence some of these artists were asked to provide further textile designs for newly founded firms or even for those such as David Whitehead, established in 1949, who were to become the most innovative firm in Britain. Eduardo Paolozzi even taught textile design from 1949 to 1955 at the Central School of Art, London, whilst continuing to design for industry. These new boldly coloured, often abstract designs, were also reflected in the new designs brought out by the wallpaper industry with designers and artists commission to design for both industries. This in turn points to another feature of the post-war attitudes towards design, where designers were not only held in a far higher regard than they had previously been but also that they were frequently to be seen designing within various decorative art fields, producing a healthy cross-fertilisation of ideas. Examples of textile pattern designs being later used on pottery, such as Terence Conran's 'Chequers' pattern for Midwinter, would have been unheard of previously.

It is precisely this innovative use of surface pattern design cleverly married to newly designed 'soft form' influenced shapes, akin to the work of Gustavsberg pottery, that played such an important part in the forthcoming 'New Look' Poole Pottery wares. Other work cited in contemporary articles points to the simplified geometric forms of Eva Zeisel as well as the monochrome fluid 'mix and match' shapes of the American Russel Wright, designed during the 1930s, (Later also developed by Kaj Franck for the Arabia Pottery, Finland,) as being important stepping stones for much of the modern 'New Look' in ceramic design. The new wares enabled Poole Pottery, once again, to become one of the leading potteries of the post-war period. In order to bring this transition about Poole Pottery underwent a programme of renewal across the board.

The Second World War caused a complete re-think at the Poole Pottery, staff numbers were greatly reduced and machinery was in desperate need of repair, as were many of the buildings, and decisions needed to be made concerning the future of the company. Even some of the decision makers had had their fill, having already given the company the best thirty years of their lives. John Adams was not a well man and Harold Stabler had died in 1945. Others left, including Ernest Baggaley, who set up his own pottery, the Branksome China Works, in the New Forest, later recruiting former staff from the Poole Pottery.

In 1945, Cyril Carter was joined by his son David, who had trained as an architect, and in the same year Roy Holland became the new works manager, having previously had ten years working in potteries in Stoke-on-Trent. It was Cyril Carter who persuaded the directors to inject investment into the ailing works, so that the Pottery could at least have a chance of rejuvenation. Whatever Cyril's argument and with the help of David Carter and Roy Holland, new buildings were erected at East Quay, although hampered by building regulations and a new tunnel kiln was installed which was fired for the first time three years after construction began in 1949.

Still under the home sales restrictions, Poole managed to revive a few overseas customers enabling them to re-introduce some two-tone Streamlined tableware, although produced with a lower lead content due to new regulations. This ware was now renamed Twintone ware and a new range, Cameo, was introduced utilising an inexpensive coloured slip, which contrasted with the white body. Other potteries were quick to catch-on to the popularity of two-tone colours, including the Denby Pottery who produced the yellow and grey Dovedale range, along with Manor Green, Cottage Blue and Homestead Brown amongst others. As the Twintone wares used expensive metallic oxide colours, John Adams also designed, in 1949, a more affordable range of tea and dinner wares; named Sherbourne, it was available in a celadon green slip or shell-pink over the white body. Another shape that was re-introduced was Wimborne, which was shown at the 1947 British Industries Fair. Numerous other wares were made during the late 1940s, all for export with a few seconds sold in Britain, mostly revivals from pre-war years, the Truda Carter floral decorated wares being such an example. By 1949 Poole was ready for full-scale mass-production with a significantly increased capacity due to the new machinery and buildings.

In 1949 John Adams, amidst great concern for the continued success of the pottery, (he having been responsible for the overall artistic direction of the Pottery) decided to retire as managing director following the successful introduction of Lucien Myers to replace him in that capacity. Filling the post of head of design was, however, going to be a more difficult task. Lucien Myers, having formerly been editor of the monthly trade journal the Pottery Gazette and Glass Trades Review, brought with him a thorough knowledge and awareness of the industry and already noticed that the American ceramics industry, through the employment of designers, many from Europe, was making rapid progress in terms of forward-thinking designs. When this was combined with the standardisation and mass-production development in the 1930s, it resulted in very affordable wares. Myers had also developed numerous useful contacts at home and abroad.

For the position of head designer, a recent young graduate from the Royal College of Art, Claude Smale, was appointed in 1950. Claude was immediately faced with task of designing commemorative wares for the Festival of Britain, although due to problems obtaining the required licence for such special products very few pieces were ever made. His next contribution, and one of his last as it turned out, was the introduction of several innovative and highly contemporary shapes, very much in the manner of the 'soft forms' formerly associated with Scandinavian pottery and even seen in some glass wares. The shapes consisted of what was described as a carafe with a rounded body and flat base with a short ringed neck, in four different sizes; some slightly swelling bodied vases with a turned-in rim, in various sizes; and a swelling round bodied vase narrowing to a slightly flared mouth, raised on a rounded foot. These shapes, which were all hand thrown in a white earthenware, are highly significant not only in terms of their contemporary look and styling but also as they formed the foundation of successive shape designs. In many respects the vases with the turned-in rims and gently rounded look towards the base are more successful, in terms of reflecting the prevalent organic softness of forms than later designs, which perhaps explains why these designs remained in production throughout the 1950s. Unfortunately,

Smale's stay was only a short one lasting about six months, and there is very little evidence as to why. Presumably, the management misjudged the complexity and depth of knowledge required in such a demanding and all encompassing position, expecting too much from a recent graduate. Certainly the next holder of the position had a great deal more experience in the field of design and was not unfamiliar with Poole Pottery.

Born in 1898, Alfred Burgess Read was 52 years old when he was appointed to head of design at Poole Pottery, having already had a very distinguished career as an industrial designer, being rewarded for his progressive designs by becoming a Royal Designer for Industry (RDI). As a recent graduate from the Royal College of Art where he had been a pupil of Harold Stabler, Read designed some kitchen tiles for Carter & Co in 1923 at the suggestion of his former teacher. A year after his appointment, in 1950, Alfred was joined at Poole by his daughter Ann Read following her graduation from the Chelsea School of Art, making her own individual contribution.

The 1950s were very much the period of the designer, in terms of individual merit, and this in turn led to the growth of independent or free lance designers, as well design groups or teams, and these designers became synonymous with the period. Amongst the leading design teams was the new Poole Pottery Design Unit under the guidance of Alfred Read, praised, at the time and by recent authors, as possibly the leading such enterprise in the Pottery industry. In reality, the design unit at Poole consisted of one main designer, Alfred Read, a thrower, Guy Sydenham and assistants who were promoted paintresses who contributed to the surface pattern designs, such as Ann Read and Ruth Pavely. Ann Read was given a free hand with her one-off or special design pieces.

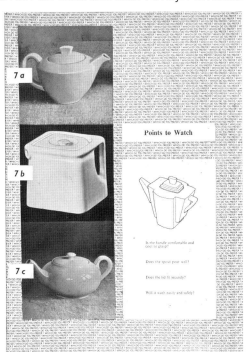

Other influential Teams or Studios included the earlier Wade Studios, under Colin Mebourne, established as a secretive trials and prototype studio. Colin Melbourne went on to produce his highly sculptural vases and animals at the experimental Beswick studio. There were also the E. Brian & Co Foley China Royal College of Art graduates, Hazel Thumpston, Maureen Tanner, Peter Cave and slightly later team leader Donald Brindley and Tom Arnold at Ridgway later joined by Enid Seeney. It could also be said that this was a significant period for the Royal College of Art, whose design graduates, the first of whom graduated in 1952, were being sought after by forward thinking industries through-out the country. The contribution to the ceramics industry from the RCA during this period was quite significant.

At Poole, the design team, in the early 1950s, also incorporated the tile side of production until the arrival of Ivor Kamlish in 1955, which will be discussed later. The other members of the team were Ruth Pavely, design

Design Quiz booklet. 1947. Illustrated is the John Adams 'Streamline' designed teapot, before alteration to the knop in 1953/5 when a button knop was added. The Streamline teapot is being heralded as 'good design', compared to the drawn image.

assistant, and Guy Sydenham, thrower, who had been at Poole since 1932. As with the other Studios or Teams in Stoke on Trent, there was a freedom of working practices within the department in which the designers could create and produce trials in an atmosphere far removed from that previously acceptable within a pottery. Donald Brindley, of E. Brain & Co for example, recalled how much of the main work force were up in arms when he and his team were allowed not to turn up for work on Saturday and even on occasion during the week, preferring instead to spend some time sketching in the gardens and conservatories of the nearby Longton Park. Such ideas derive from the studio environment established by continental and Scandinavian potteries.

One of Alfred Read's first tasks was to redevelop the in-glaze colour palette used at Poole to achieve a contemporary look to be used with new pattern designs. It wasn't long before new shapes, adding to those already designed by Smale, were developed, including gourd forms, bottle vases, broad open dishes and open conical vases. As if to emphasise contemporary influences on the new designs by Alfred Read, Ruth Pavely and Guy Sydenham their wares were often exhibited on and against textile and wallpaper designs, as well as around contemporary furniture that enhanced the look of the exhibits. In 1953 a collection of the new wares was exhibited at the Tea Centre in Regent Street, London, with monochrome wares, Coronation pieces, Twintone wares and the rhythmical fabric-and-wallpaper-inspired abstract repeat patterns by Read, all set against contemporary fabric designs, one in particular entitled 'Fall' by Lucienne Day. At the same venue only five years later, the backdrop for similar wares along with the new 'Freeform' wares, were textiles inspired by the abstract artist Jackson Pollock, 'Oak' designed by Dorothy Carr for Heal's and with 'Projection' by Françoise Lelong, also for Heal's. Studying numerous advertising, promotional and related photographs and illustrations during the 1950s, it immediately becomes apparent how important the background settings, exhibition stands and furniture are in order to create overall appeal and the 'contemporary' look. Contemporary magazines and professional magazines were also seen as important promotional opportunities and were used as such by Lucien Myers, Cyril Carter and Read. If only part of the larger marketing ploy, these promotional articles, advertising and inclusion in the contemporary Design Quiz brochures and even television programmes did much to elevate Poole Pottery wares above their contemporary manufacturers.

The Poole design unit kept on producing numerous new designs, keeping the wares looking fresh and up to date, as well as beating any competition or mimics within the industry. By the second half of the 1950s there were many firms in all the decorative arts fields who started to produce thinly veiled imitations and even copies of the 'New Look', often referred to as new 'Lookalikes', a term coined by Lesley Jackson. This particularly affected the ceramics firms and fabric companies. The 'Lookalikes' products often being badly made with little thought for colour balance, shape or overall composition, most degenerating into 'kitsch'. One of the ways around this, systematically used by Roy Midwinter at the Midwinter pottery, was to keep producing new fresh designs as fast as possible either through internal designers or external commissions. In any event, this tactic suited the high fashion wares that would by their nature have a short shelf life, unlike the traditional wares that consumers bought to last a long time.

At Poole the conventionally decorated ware, the tried and tested 'traditional' designs were brought up to date. Truda Adams's (later Truda Carter having married Cyril Carter in 1930) floral patterns were still highly popular having over been for many years become an established good seller for Poole. The designs were re-worked, becoming harsher and in many respects simpler, than the pre-war designs. The body itself also changed due to technological advances in the search for an even more refined body and smoother glaze. As a result, the body became thinner and the glaze noticeably whiter, (it was called alpine white), although there were also some variations in glaze colours available, such as a pearl grey. These wares found growing markets in America, Australia, the West Indies, the Far East and elsewhere. New shapes were added to fulfil demand. Changing life styles and home environments demanded such forms as hors d'oeuvres sets, often painted with stylised fish, crabs and related aquatic life or indeed flowers, table lamps, cheese dishes, ashtrays, display boxes and cruets sets. In 1951, before the lifting of restrictions, the tablelamps were inventively produced by joining two slop bowls at their rims and adding holes for the electrical fittings and the wire.

Between 1955 and 1956 Ann Read was producing some remarkable, free-hand designs meant for limited production. There are in the region of fifty-five plaques, each numbered, dated and signed, which were produced in various sizes and shapes and using a black ground, an alpine white ground and one or two others. Ann Read's special fiftieth anniversary plate design for Cyril Carter, 1905-55, named 'Yaffle Hill' after Cyril's house is another well recorded design of the period, as is her special bamboo patterned Streamline table ware service design for Heal's, dating from 1956. This series of designs can be seen as a continuation of the individualistic approach to design normally associated with former free-lance designers, such as Olive Bourne and Leslie Ward, and harks back to the artistic flair of Truda Adams, Erna Manners and Margaret Holder.

From 1956 the Poole Pottery design team issued a new set of shapes and patterns that were clearly ground-breaking in terms of British industrial ceramic wares; these were the 'Freeforms' designed by Alfred Read and Guy Sydenham, although Read conceived the forms. The soft, rhythmic shapes and patterns of the early 1950s 'contemporary' wares gave way to highly sculptural forms, based on ideas derived from the zoomorphic vases by Picasso whose work was highly promoted and discussed in the early 1950s, through to works by Richard Ginori, the 'California West Coast look', as well as sculptural works by Henry Moore. Similar influences of this period can be seen in the work of Colin Melbourne for John Beswick, promoted as the 'CM' series to match the contemporary scene', as well as designs by Tibor Reich for the Joseph Bourne, Denby Pottery. Wares were also produced at the Midwinter Pottery, Carlton ware works, Wade, Heath & Co and Pilkington's Royal Lancastrian Pottery designed by the American born Mitzi Cunnliffe.

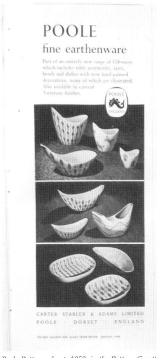

Poole Pottery advert, 1959, in the Pottery Gazette and Glass Trades Review. illustrating the Contemporary wares.

The surface pattern designs in the second half of the 1950s were produced in even greater numbers and frequency, the free form shapes hand-painted with often very simple repeated motifs, produced in various colour-ways and scale to match the size of the piece, or in boldly coloured monochrome glazes. Contrasting plain glazes such as black panther, magnolia white, lime yellow and red Indian were typical of the harlequin look of the period, numerous vases often being purchased to be arranged for the colour combinations. The more simple the hand-painted pattern the faster wares and more inexpensively the wares could be produced. The fact that the shapes were designed to be slip-cast further increased the rate of production, consistency and reduced costs. At the same time the quality was assured and the high standards maintained with the skills of the paintresses being paramount.

On occasion even rarer studio pieces that were meant as trial or one-off pieces can be fond. These often have an even more exaggerated hand-thrown shape and tended to use more variations and colours. Such pieces were shown, indeed made for exhibition, at various venues in the late 1950s, including the Regent Street Tea Centre in London, as mentioned earlier. Conversely, numerous new shapes were made in the freeform range for ordinary domestic use together with the new highly abstract patterns, moving even further away from the previously acceptable and well-established 'traditional' patterned wares. Such pieces included cheese dishes, cucumber dishes, jam pots, cruets sets, hostess or television sets, numerous small dishes and ashtrays.

For many in the pottery industry, indeed many consumers, Poole Pottery in the 1950s made some quite startling changes to the traditionally accepted style of its work, but even more was to come. In 1956 Ann Read became unwell and had to leave the pottery. Her father, having had tuberculosis the year before and whilst recuperating come up with the 'free form' shapes, continued for another year, retiring in 1958. In the same year Robert Jefferson applied and was appointed to the post vacated by Alfred Read. Robert Jefferson was a product of Professor Baker's closer links with industry strategy, producing designers specially suited for industrial requirements, at the Royal College of Art where he was in charge of ceramics. Robert managed the Odney Pottery at Cookham for the John Lewis Partnership, as well as executing freelance designs for Minton, Ridgway and table wares for the Orient line before taking on the position of lecturer of ceramics at the Stoke-on-Trent School of

Art in 1956, having earlier worked at the Bullers studio. This new role as head of design for Poole Pottery was in fact something Robert had long wished for and for the next eight years was to prove a high point in his career as well as a significant period for Poole Pottery.

During this period Robert Jefferson's most important contribution at Poole was to shift the emphasis towards everyday functional tablewares, not only with the introduction of new shapes and types of ware but also the use of mass-production methods of decoration and manufacture. He later made important developments to the concept of the Studio, in it's broader meaning, with the introduction of numerous designers who were allowed far more freedom to create and execute their own work within the parameters of the Poole Studio.

In his second year at Poole, having taken a year to straighten out various issues that needed to have a homogenous look to them, from promotional leaflet designs, display boards, advertising and the showrooms, Robert designed

Poole Pottery advert, 1960, in the Pottery Gazette and Glass Trades Review. This advert is promoting the printed Pebble pattern by Robert Jefferson, designed in 1959, applied using a Murray Curvex machine. Notice the rather retrogressive Grays Pottery design below as well as the different approaches to advertising.

the Contour range, his first significant statement of the future direction of the pottery as he saw it. The Contour shape with its distinctive wide, open up-swept handle and rounded compressed shape was an immediate success, selling in some of the Twintone colours as well as with a new Pebble pattern created using the new Murray-Curvex off-set printing machine. The 1959 Pebble pattern, produced in black or grey, was an early indication of the way Poole Pottery production was headed. The new pattern received unreserved praise in the trade journals, although this was the only pattern produced by Poole using the technique. The 'Murray Machine', as it was advertised, involved the use of a 'gelatine bomb' to mechanically transfer a pattern from an inked copper plate etched with the design, taken up by the 'bomb' and transferred to an object. The nature of the 'bomb' meant that the design could be applied perfectly, with no creases or joins associated with the use of multiple and/or single transfer prints. Its limitations were that it was only really suitable for flat or gently curved wares, such as the popular American influenced 'scoop' forms which were currently fashionable. With difficulty other forms could be made to fit, such as a tureen cover, a hole being cut into the pendulous 'bomb' in order for the pattern to cleverly start under the knob and over the entire surface of the cover. Another well-known use of this technique is the Enid Seeney 'Homemaker' pattern for Ridgway & Adderley dating to about the same time.

The growing informality of eating habits in much of Britain, Europe and America, together with an increasing desire to eat culinary dishes from abroad, largely as a consequence of the growing continental holiday market, saw the introduction of new types of vessels for cooking and serving meals in the 1960s. Stoneware was rapidly becoming the fastest selling pottery material compared to china and earthenware, particularly in America and France, where firms such as Joseph Bourne of Derbyshire were selling their Denby ranges very successfully. The image of the sturdy cooking vessel, eating hand prepared fresh vegetables and being able to serve from the vessel in which the meal was cooked, was what the consumer wanted. Later into the 1970s other potteries began to make inroads into the market, with Midwinter selling their 'Stonehenge' ranges, made to look like stoneware even though they were made of earthenware. Portmeirion also enjoyed strong American and British sales.

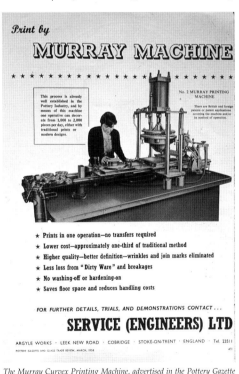

The Murray Curvex Printing Machine, advertised in the Pottery Gazette & Glass Trades Review, 1958.

In 1960, Robert Jefferson was able to introduce this new style of 'oven-to-table' ware at the Poole Pottery, largely because little alteration was needed to the body of the ware already being made as the firing temperature for the earthenware was already higher than normal. Two new designs were developed for the new range, Lucullus and Herb Garden, each combined with a solid colour of 'Blue Moon', a pale yellow, 'Celeste' and 'Heather Rose', although the latter was dropped early on. What is significant about these designs was that they were applied as silk-screen prints, in themselves quite innovatory, directly onto the raw unfired glaze, resulting in permanent in-glaze decoration. Robert also designed special packaging for these wares, something several forward thinking potteries, such as Midwinter, were also promoting. However the retailers had problems finding storage so the ideas were put on hold. Selling boxed sets of ware was something for which firms such as the Susie Cooper pottery had long been acknowledged. Equally it was Susie Cooper who was a very keen not only to promote functional aspects of tea, coffee and dinner wares, but also showed a remarkable awareness of the problems of storing large sets of dinner, tea and coffee wares. Susie Cooper had patented her stackable and reversible tureen lids on her Kestrel shape as early as 1934, indicating that it was important for ceramic designers to consider aspects of storage creating as part of the design, wares that could be stacked. Robert Jefferson in his next tableware design, Compact, 1965, showed his concerns on this area, although the lids, deliberately made without a knop for further stacking, were later redesigned by Tony Morris in 1969.

Robert Jefferson, on a more utilitarian level, also created highly successful gift wares such as the famous leaping dolphin models which can still be bought today (Although modified over the years). He also created numerous other designs, such as the table lamps for Helios with their cylindrical or square pottery bases and numerous preserve jars, boxes and vases all hand thrown in his Bokhara range in 1964. In the same year various moulded wall plaques and trays, in the form of fish, birds and a knife were designed and others depicting a mermaid or a castle were also made. The idea behind these pieces came from a visit to Vallauris during his first years at Poole, encouraged by Lucien Myers, and another visit to the Arabia studios in Finland (as part of an organised trip to Scandinavia by the Design and Industries Association). Robert also travelled to America, seeing for himself the prevailing styles of the day. These designs reflected the demands of the consumer of the period with ever changing life styles. Equally Robert's early individual studio wares exhibited at the Regent Street Tea Centre in London in 1961 not only reflected current contemporary interests in studio pottery but also indicated something of what was being planned for future developments at the Poole Pottery Studio.

Regeneration

1960 to 1980

The 1960s had seen a growing interest and heightened awareness amongst the public of studio pottery. Often discussed and often vilified in the British press and ceramics trade press studio pottery was either dismissed as being irrelevant 'Picasettes' (imitators of Picasso) or irrelevant in terms of commercial pottery, the latter having had their fill of what they saw as government backing for studio pottery since the War. Even so, amongst some of the public, studio pottery fulfilled certain criteria related to attitudes in line with a new lifestyle with earthy associations that were relevant to the openness and freedom of thought of the period. This formed an important foundation for what in recent years has become increasingly recognised as a highly significant contribution by Poole Pottery to the 1960s and 1970s British ceramic scene.

Launched in October 1963 at Heals', London, with a new special back stamp by Robert Jefferson, the Poole Pottery 'Studio' carried on a long tradition within Poole Pottery of not only employing artists and designers, both internally and externally, but also, through such initiative, staying at the forefront of contemporary ceramic design. The inauguration of the studio was arguably one of the most significant post-War contributions made by a British Pottery and one that certainly elevated Poole pottery to one of the most forward thinking contemporary potteries. The Poole studio wares and overall philosophy were very different to the Midwinter Pottery, another major innovative firm of the day. At Poole there was a vast amount of experimental work carried out, mainly on glazes, and the introduction of avant-garde hand-painted designs meant that no two pieces were ever the same. The team had a far greater creative freedom more akin to that of an individual studio potter or fine artist but working within the confines of a commercial concern. Other contemporary commercial potteries during the 1960s and into the 1970s employed studio potters to design ranges with limited success, not having the historical association between employing numerous artists and designers that was such a normal procedure at Poole.

Initially developed by Robert Jefferson and Guy Sydenham, this duo were joined in 1963 by Tony Morris who graduated from the Newport School of Art in fine arts and who contributed to the technical side of the studio as well as to the design side. Tony Morris was recruited for his painting skills and inventive flair which is easy to detect in the works he executed. As the Studio developed, more paintresses from the pottery and recent graduates from the local School of Art joined the team, everyone being encouraged to add their own individual statements to the shape and pattern designs. Christine Tate, Elizabeth Hayne, Betty Bantten, Shirley Campbell, Jennifer Wiles, Margaret Anderson, Thelma Bush, Carole Holden, and Geraldine O'Meara were amongst those who joined the studio in the early years, Christine Tate becoming design assistant and later a supervisor.

The earliest wares developed by the studio were marketed under the name Delphis, which initially included the individual hand thrown studio wares of Guy Sydenham, etc. Later around 1970 Delphis came to represent in the eye of the public just the brightly coloured orange, red, green and yellow glazes. As these colours were also the least costly and most stable, they became the standardised production under the Delphis name. The designs were gaudy, bold and abstract, reflecting contemporary painting and sculpture as well as the hallucinogenic and psychedelic experimentation of the late 1960s period. Similar design influences can be seen in textile designs of the period.

The earlier Delphis shapes were far more varied and numerous than the later, more standardised, wares. Guy Sydenham and others created exaggerated compressed ovoid vases and tall gently tapering vases, whilst some shapes were compressed cylinders with sharp under cuts to the neck and/or base. The shapes were often heavily cut, faceted in a band or cross-hatched with vertical lines, other pieces being carved and cut with anything from abstract patterns or images to stylised sun faces, fish, birds, sea animals, landscapes or sheep. These wares were a significant move away from the Studio pottery inspired wares that Robert Jefferson had produced in the early 1960s, which largely picked up on the prevalent interest in black and white decorated wares developed from the so called 'Picasettes' studio potters, as well as the interest in Op art. The glazes used on these wares were initially based on previously known and used glazes at the pottery and it was only after a number of years that additional mixtures were bought in. A large proportion of the early pieces show the distinctive flair and imagination of Tony Morris, particularly the sun faces, sun spots and heavily abstract designs with arrangements of blocks of colour and shapes. Experimentation and individual designs were the norm.

Such luxuries could only exist because of the support and profits from the more commercial side of the business, and Robert Jefferson had done much to develop this side. That the studio and even the everyday wares produced by the pottery were allowed to continue in this way is all the more surprising given that, in the midst of this renewed energy and growth, Poole Pottery was taken over, although the word 'merger' was used at the time and by subsequent critics, in 1964. Take-over is a more realistic assessment with the later complete transition of board members in favour of Pilkington's. Pilkington's, however, were more interested in the healthy tile side of the business which had been such competition to them for many years. True to their word, Pilkington's injected much needed capital into the domestic and decorative side of the business seeing the value of the financial contribution made by Poole Pottery. Such largess was almost certainly due to the fact that the board members of Pilkington's realised the value of the pottery side having earlier in the century been amongst the numerous producers of even more lavish ranges of Art Pottery themselves.

Even with the potential for growth as a consequence of the take-over, all was not well at the management level. In the year preceding the take-over, in 1963, Lucien Myers, for so long an ardent advocate and driving force of the artistic side of the pottery as well as an ingenious promoter and salesman of Poole wares, resigned. The position of managing director was filled by Roy Holland, who would have found it hard to match the passion and drive of his predecessor, even if he had been given the freedom to do so. In the same year, Cyril Carter, the last member in a continuous Carter family line, retired from the board, leaving the company altogether two years later. The departures of both Cyril and Lucien following the long negotiations with Pilkington's inevitably brought about change. The outward appearance was one of growth and development but the spirit, internal support and inherent trust following years of careful management were instantly and inevitably swept aside with the take-over. In many respects, even following the much needed artistic input of figures such as Tony Morris, Guy Sydenham and Christine Tate, the departure of Robert Jefferson in 1965, having seemingly "designed himself out of a job", was another huge blow to the pottery. For some unknown reason Robert Jefferson was not replaced, perhaps due to the new management imposing some new financial constraints or being unappreciative of the need for a full-time co-ordinating designer.

Whatever the course of events or the thinking at management level the pottery kept going with new machinery and top-hat kilns which, consequently, created increased demands in terms of production. The Studio, established by Robert Jefferson, was reorganised to include both a shop and a new visitors centre, largely in an effort to free the working pottery of the hordes of visitors that used to descend. The new-look studio, renamed the Craft Section, was also to include traditional wares as well as the Studio ranges. The paintresses were still very much encouraged to produce their own designs and this they did. Christine Tate recalls how she "originated many of the designs and other girls filled in the colour (then) putting their mark on the base." This further emphasises the anonymity of the designers in the Studio or Craft section.

During the late 1960s experimentation was still very much encouraged with new 'outside' colours and glazes being used in increasing amounts. Following a visit to Vallauris by Guy Sydenham, the new senior craftsman, and Tony Morris, in 1966, the vital colours red and orange that were to form the basis for the standardisation of the Delphis range, were discovered. Initially red glazes had been developed from a by-product of sulphuric acid and orange was formed from Uranium. These colours were replaced by the safer and commercially available Zircon encapsulated Cadmium and Selenium. Christine Tate mentions that the uranium orange was very difficult to fire, the glaze tending to burn to a darker shade or to blister and even peel if the consistency was wrong. Christine also recalls there being a wide range of colours available for the individual wares with new colours being added from glaze manufacturers. Magnolia white, which was used from the beginning on the backs of plates and inside vases, also became problematic being replaced in 1966 by a clear Crystal glaze producing a slightly matte appearance.

The Delphis range become very popular selling particularly well in Japan, America and Canada, amongst other foreign countries, which led to a standardisation in 1971 of the best selling colours, namely orange, bold red, green and yellow, as well as a cobalt blue. The number of pieces in the range was also reduced, again for commercial reasons, but in terms of production the wares were so popular that they were still in produced in 1980. Over the years some fifty-eight shapes were used for Delphis wares although only eight were produced for the full period. Sometime in the early 1970s, probably after Pilkington's was taken over by the Thomas Tilling Group in 1971, piece rates were brought in at Poole, initially for the Delphis paintresses, in an effort again to speed up production but at the cost of quality. By 1973 Delphis was being promoted as 'gift' ware along with ordinary 'traditional' wares indicating the reduced status of the wares within the pottery.

The new Aegean and Atlantis ranges, however, were given a higher status. The Aegean range was introduced in 1970 having been developed in the previous year by Leslie Elsden, the master of the spray glazing technique. Spray glazing had been introduced as part of the production process in the 1930s, taking over from hand-dipping, and was seen to best effect of the Picotee wares. The Aegean range, based on the spraying technique, initially involved six 'special' methods of decoration in 1969, but only five were in evidence at the time of production in the following year, the five being, silhouette, sgraffito, mosaic, flow-line and carved. It was the former two techniques that were the most popular. The silhouette technique involved the use of a liquid rubber resist which was painted on to form the pattern, often after the pattern outline had been pounced onto the piece, then sprayed over in a colour which was allowed to dry before the rubber was peeled off and the piece fired. Flowline produced a streaked and/or mottled effect through the overlaying and interaction of two coloured glazes, the result being similar to the dripped harmony wares of Shelley or the Delecia glaze wares of the Wilkinson factory, whist mosaic, as the name suggests, produced a mosaic-like abstract pattern or picture through the use of different blocks or areas of colours separated by resist lines. Some of the decorative techniques used on the Delphis wares were much the same, especially on some of the more one-off experimental studio wares, although there was a far greater degree of hand-painting involved. Some of the Aegean pieces were very complex, involving several layers or areas of colour which were then either carved through or involved different coloured segmented spray-glazed areas which were then sgraffitoed through. These pieces initially known as 'extra special' Aegean were called Ionian after March 1974 and by June the remaining unassociated patterns, including the signs of the Zodiac, knight in armour, and the complex landscapes were all withdrawn.

Amongst the contemporary potteries, mainly based in Stoke-on-Trent, there were very few that could match the variety, innovation and artistic individuality of Poole Pottery. Susan Williams-Ellis, daughter of Sir Clough Williams-Ellis, owner of the extraordinary Italianate styled village of Portmeirion on the Llyn peninsular in North Wales, took over the A E Gray Pottery, Stoke on Trent, in 1959, later merging it with the Kirkham Pottery to form the Portmeirion Potteries. Susan Williams-Ellis started to produce some highly individual designs, mainly for sale at the Italian village, which reflected the fashion for bright and bold colours, abstract pattern and form as well as exaggeration of shapes. Colin Melbourne produced some highly sculptural and abstract wares for the Crown Devon pottery under the name 'Memphis', which seems to owe much to Aztec artefacts and the taste for bold extremes of shape and line, with the added hint of exotic lavishness. There were a few other designers employed by pottery firms who were again give some freedom to produce fashionable wares expressing contemporary high street fashion. Robert Minkin, for example, designed tall cylindrical coffee sets for Wedgwood, Barabra Brown designed surface patterns for Midwinter. Susie Cooper reflecting her extraordinary versatility, design skills and awareness of contemporary trends, not to mention longevity, produced numerous highly popular designs for Wedgwood (who had by this time taken over the Susie Cooper China works), ranging from stylised floral designs to highly abstract geometric patterns. Today Susie Cooper's innovative, indeed pioneering use of lithography to produce patterns such as 'Diablo', 'Gay Stripes', 'Harlequinade' and 'Pennant', as well as the floral designs 'Corn Poppy', 'Iris', 'Florida', etc, are all highly regarded as typifying contemporary fashion trends and are highly collectable today. Her 'Can' shaped coffee cup is still in production at Wedgwood some forty years after it was first designed.

The third style or type of ware produced in the Craft Section during this period, Atlantis, was the most avant garde on the commercial pottery side. Initiated by Robert Jefferson but fully developed and enlarged upon by Guy Sydenham from 1969, these wares had more in common with contemporary studio pottery and in some respects hark back to the earliest experimental lustre wares of Owen Carter, between 1900 and 1918. Guy Sydenham who had been living with his family on a surplus Royal Navy MTB torpedo boat on Long Island in Poole Harbour, moved to another island, Green Island, in 1968, where he established his own small pottery. Looking at much of the Atlantis wares with this added knowledge about Guy Sydenham's domestic arrangements immediately brings a greater understanding of the some of the influences seen in the wares. The gauged, stippled and sgraiffitoed surfaces of many of the vessels start to reflect the barnacles, pebbles, aquatic foliage and crustaceans that were such an everyday experience for him. Where the hand thrown and sometimes coloured bodied pieces have been glazed, Guy used a variety of techniques, such as combining glazes of differing viscosity to produce a reactive effect, to further enhance the marine visual effect of his pieces. After 1971 all the Atlantis pieces were marked with a capital 'A' to indicate that they were Atlantis designs, as if they weren't distinctive enough, and continued to be produced until 1979, some three years after Guy Sydenham had resigned.

The 1970s saw a general renewed interest in stoneware as a material, the emphasis supposedly on the hand made 'truth of materials' attributes. Stoneware often being used as rather a loose definition to include wares that 'looked' like or that apparently had the attributes of stoneware. The previous decade had already seen a growth in the number of people buying hand-made Studio Pottery as a form of non-conformist self-expression. Denby Pottery of Joseph Bourne & Co, Derbyshire, were one of the successful stoneware firms to emerge during this period making a wide variety of durable and functional wares with patterns reflecting the 'back to earth' qualities of clay as a material. There was also a growing interest in and presentation of gastronomic dishes from new 'foreign' countries. Midwinter, following a few set-backs in the late 1960s, returned with a new 'Stonehenge' range of shapes and a suitably speckled glaze, 'Creation', which made there fine earthenware body have all the appearance of stoneware. What was particularly noticeable during 1960s and even more so during the 1970s, was the huge increase in wares made for the export markets in North America, Canada, Japan and Australia. Midwinter, Denby, Susie Cooper designs for Wedgwood, Martin Hunt designs for Hornsea and Poole Pottery were very active in all of these markets each vying for space with continental and other manufacturers, such as Rosenthal, Noritake, Richard-Ginori and Villeroy and Boch, amongst others, with many new ranges being specifically designed and only sold in the export markets.

It was against this background that the New Stoneware tableware ranges designed by Tony Morris and Guy Sydenham were made and exported from the late 1960s through to the 1970s, albeit in fairly limited numbers. Throughout this same period Robert Jefferson, following a special commission, designed the Compact range which was in production, from 1965 to 1992, and was augmented by a new Jefferson design in 1979 called Style. The late 1970s were a very diverse and somewhat confusing period for Poole with the opening up of seemingly endless new trends, styles and potential markets, the huge potential of export markets becoming increasingly significant.

The 1970s for Poole Pottery had seen it's usual comings and goings with centenary celebrations in 1973 to mark the establishment of the pottery, the take-over by the Thomas Tilling Group of Pilkington's and the managing director Roy Holland retiring in 1976 ushering in Trevor Wright as his replacement. In the same year, 1979, Guy Sydenham resigned following some exhaustive years battling to preserve the integrity of the Poole Studio, and fighting against the implementation of 'piece rate' working and for the continued freedom of self-expression in the studio, amongst other concerns. In the end the commercial concerns and interests of the new owners in a highly competitive business meant a change of direction and emphasis. In about 1979 the Craft section declined rapidly finally closing in 1982, the high costs involved in such intensive hand production wares becoming too great. No doubt there are innumerable reasons why the closure occurred but in the end change is always necessary indeed healthy for the continued success of any company. Whether the Craft section was being heavily subsidised by the commercial side of production or whether it was market forces that determined the change perhaps only time will tell. As if to mark the significance of the closure, Poole Pottery was honoured in that year with a Royal visit by Queen Elizabeth II and the Duke of Edinburgh, a fitting mark of former glories and achievements over the previous century.

Modernisation

1980 to Present

The 1980s heralded a very significant change at Poole Pottery; one that the Pottery did not always seem very comfortable with. The heavy bias towards giftwares, the introduction of an entirely new body, bone china, and the closure of the Craft section with the consequent loss and redeployment of staff, must have caused an unsettled feeling. It should be remembered that throughout the 1970s and 1980s the Traditional hand painted range was, of course, still being produced and formed a large part of production stability along with the various tableware ranges.

Political and social issues changed again in the depression of late 1970s and early 1980s with the tightening of financial purses due to a hike in the cost of oil, high interest rates, as well as high unemployment and capping of wages. The 1970s can be seen as a transitional period with a diversity and plethora of styles, which was reigned in to some extent, with a new direction taken up by 1980. What it meant as far as most potteries were concerned was a reduction in the number and range of pieces being made, thereby reducing production costs, and the use of a wider range of patterns on the limited number of wares being produced. This was not the solution for all pottery firms. Those at the top end of production concentrated even more on the expensive end of production, producing new, innovative and expensive wares for those wanting something with more individuality or recognisably different.

The influence as far as Poole Pottery was concerned saw the Studio/Craft productions peter out with the 'Sienna', 'Contrast' and 'Calypso' showing the last vestiges with the Elsden reactive glazes and spray glazing techniques. Ros Sommerfelt's 'Olympus' range emphasised the concerns of reducing the costs involved in production, not only by reducing the number of shapes in the range but also by making use of a decorative technique that only needed to be fired once.

The new team, promoted within the pottery, of Ros Sommerfelt, Alan White, Alan Clarke and Elaine Williamson started to take shape. Tony Morris was one of the last of the Craft team to depart during this period, leaving in 1982. Alan White took over from Guy Sydenham and is still at the pottery today. The introduction of printed patterns and high volume selling shapes such as mugs, numerous new vases, table lamps, trinket boxes and other such dressing table and decorative bathroom wares showed the way ahead for the new look Poole Pottery.

New lines were introduced by Ros Sommerfelt including the Art Nouveau inspired 'Beardsley' range and revivalist 'Camelot' plates. Although the 'Beardsley' range was produced using printed patterns on slip-cast wares, pre-requisites for mass-production, there were hand thrown vessels made in the early stages of development. Printed patterns and slip cast wares were now the norm, the surface decorations often indicative of the desire amongst the buying public for something 'quintessentially English rural', floral or simple and timeless. Elaine Williamson was now responsible for steering the new team during the 1980s designing the highly popular 'Concert' tableware range which lasted until 1992. In typical Poole tradition the outside partnership of Queensberry Hunt first became involved with the Poole pottery designing the Flair range, 1983 to 1986, followed by the Astral tableware range, 1989 to 1990. The Queensberry Hunt partnership also designed a range of vases, 'Calypso' and 'Cello', each with various glaze effects and patterns, as well as some lamp bases, 'Corinthian', all during the 1980s. Other external designers also contributed to the production with Robin Welsh designing the 'Campden' range in 1989 to 1991. The 'Aztec' range of vases, decorated with a simplistic printed band, was introduced by Liane Hutchings of Mary Jones Design in 1988-89.

The new fast growing limited edition market which had seen the introduction of the Tony Morris designed Medieval calendar plates, in 1972 and the Cathedral plates in 1973 saw the introduction of new lines at Poole. One such new line was the production of animal figures by Barbara Linley Adams, as well as her limited edition plates. It wasn't long before the many of the ever growing number of Linley stoneware animals began to be made in bone china, the same material also used to produce the six elegant figurines, Katherine, Elizabeth, Abigail, Victoria and Lillie, each decorated with printed floral patterns and gilding. Other modellers such as Bert Baggaley introduced or remodelled numerous other animals, including the famous leaping dolphins, the single models having been designed by Robert Jefferson and the double models by Tony Morris. The move into bone china production was an inevitable part of the change in direction of the gift ware market. By the mid 1980s Elaine Williamson and Ros Sommerfelt were producing trinket boxes, vases and ashtrays with on-glaze transfer printed patterns such as' Iona', 'Athena', 'Ophelia', 'Cymbeline' and 'Trelissick'.

The late 1980s brought with it yet another shift in emphasis due to better market forces and a freeing of the restrained purse strings of the early 1980s. The new direction of Poole can be seen in the 'Dorset Fruit' pattern designed by Alan Clarke in 1990, which was inspired by the blue sponged wares of the external designers Hinchcliffe and Barber dating from 1986. Yet again, it was the willingness, indeed openness of Poole Pottery to use external designers, still after all this time something alien to most traditional potteries of Stoke-on-Trent, that brought about a significant development for Poole. The 'Dorset Fruit' collection and subsequent sponged and stencilled patterns enabled the Poole Pottery to enter yet another significant period in the history of firm, just before its centenary celebrations.

In October 1992 Peter Mills led a team of like-minded individuals in a management buy-out of the Poole Pottery from the parent company. Today it is still under the same control. The most immediate visual public impact of the change was seen at the International Trade Fair, 1993, held at the NEC on the outskirts of Birmingham, where an impressive new stand had been designed showing off to great effect many new ranges. Since 1992 much has changed or rather largely reverted to how it used to be. The Poole Studio has been re-established largely due the very healthy market conditions that prevail today. Higher wages and very low unemployment in a generally cash rich society which wants to expresses itself in a more individual and expressive way has meant this can happen. The return to the more diversified and eclectic tastes of the International market and its continuing demand for greater choice has enabled the lavish, high quality wares that develop from the studio environment to be seen on the open market.

Initially the new artistic direction was guided by David Queensberry, who was appointed Art Director at Poole in 1992, following a lengthy involvement with numerous potteries in the 1970s and 1980s, including Poole, after his position as Professor at the Royal College of Art in London. New young designers were brought in and a more focused approach was taken towards potential future markets which reflected new production and marketing strategies that had been going on in America, with firms such as Noritake. Tableware production, now reflecting a more informal or casual manner of dining, has taken over as the dominant part of commercial production with the gift ware markets still eagerly sought after. In 1995 new distributors were appointed in Australia and New Zealand, with new growth in the Japanese and Korean markets. Market research highlighted certain areas to develop, one being the bridal market, in 1995 Poole was third on the Bridal Registry list at Bloomingdales, in New York City. The American market saw a particularly strong growth in the demand for Poole wares with the Alfama design by Anita Harris being made exclusively for Tiffany's. Amongst the new internal designers Anita Harris's designs have proven to be particularly popular, her designs often harking back to traditional tried and tested vine leaf motifs and simple, yet highly effective, floral designs. Other notable designs have been contributed by Kate Byrne, particularly 'Orchard' together with designs by Sarah Chalmers and Nicola Wiehaln. Externally designs have been contributed by Rachel Barker, Andrew Brickett and Fenella Mallalieu, their designs often using a combination of traditional techniques in a simple cost effective manner. Some of the general designs more obviously reflect the concentrated effort on certain markets in particular the use of late nineteenth century seed packet designs as transfer prints. All the time the management has sought special orders for certain retailers, chain stores and institutions such as the National Trust, creating special or exclusive designs for the clients. Old techniques have been re-introduced to great effect, especially the spray glazed or air brushed designs of Alan Clarke, a pupil of Leslie Elsden. The Craft studio concept has even been revived through the work of Alan White who returned to Poole Pottery in 1983, having been made redundant a few years previously, to run his own Studio making and selling his own wares until 1992 when he was taken on by the new management to work on special projects. Today Alan, who originally joined Poole in 1966 training under Guy Sydenham, continues to make one-off and limited edition pieces, still in his studio within a pottery, highlighting not only his individual style but also the influence of the local marine and pastoral environment.

Perhaps the most significant revival in recent years and one that is synonymous with the history of Poole Pottery, is the establishment of the new Poole Studio, in keeping with a long association with the in-house designer or team of designers. The new Poole Studio was launched with the arrival of Sally Tuffin, in 1995, following her experiences at the Moorcroft Pottery, having brought life back to that ailing pottery after it nearly collapsed in the hands of some unsympathetic commercial pottery owners, as well working at her own Dennis China Works. The launch of the studio went hand in hand with another new venture, one seemingly symptomatic of the 1980s and 1990s, namely the inauguration of the Poole Pottery Collectors Club. Again symptomatic of the public's growing awareness of the historical impact and interest in the Poole Pottery was the publication of Leslie Hayward's long awaited new book on Poole Pottery. Leslie had had a very long association with Poole Pottery, two of his great uncles having worked with the Dressler tunnel kiln before World War One and Leslie himself having worked at Poole since 1950 until his retirement. Even then, Leslie returned as honorary curator of the factory museum due to his extensive knowledge of the Poole Pottery, and this was where he could still be found until recently.

Sally Tuffin's 'Strolling Leopard' year vase, 1995, was the first of the 'exclusive to members' wares to be produced, followed in 1996 by the 'Forest Deer' vase and the 1997 Brede class 'Poole Lifeboat' plate. Members who manage to attend what has become the annual Gala Day are also able to order special commemorative dishes. Other special pieces were exclusively offered to members such as the 'Yaffle' plate, 1996, as well as the 'Parasol' vase and bowl, 1996, both designs by Sally Tuffin. Other designs from the Studio by Sally Tuffin were available to the wider public, such as 'Seagull', 'Bird' and 'Fish' but in a remarkable high-flying publicity scoop Sally's 'Blue Poole' design will take some beating in years to come. Calling the commission "the biggest coup of the year so far," Peter Mills was somewhat understating the case as British Airways commissioned and accepted Sally's 'Blue Poole' design, painted by Karen Brown, to decorate the tail fin of one of their aircraft, as well as inscribing the name on the nose of the plane. The design also appeared on other planes, "Jumbos and smaller regional aircraft", as well as "airline stationery, ticket wallets, menu cards, etc." This commission exemplifies part of the new approach to marketing and increasing the public profile of the pottery, commissions being taken on from numerous sources. Today it is the work of Karen Brown, who arrived in 1996 working for Sally Tuffin, who has risen to prominence within the Poole Studio, her Isle of Purbeck wares proving to be very popular. Karen's 'Corfe Castle' design has caused just as much interest as the original 'Viking', followed by the 'Old Harry', 'Lotus' and 'Caro' designs, with some of these designs being produced in limited numbers. Karen has also production limited edition pieces including the 'Ocean Liner' plate in 1998. Some of the latest designs to come from Poole include two 'Classic Art Deco' vases, small and large, both pieces being hand-thrown and hand-painted, borrowing heavily from former Poole Pottery designs by Truda Carter in the early 1930s. The larger vase, 20 centimetres high, is being produced in a Limited Edition of 100 whilst the smaller vase, 12 centimetres, has an edition of 150.

Peter Mills, again learning from the company's illustrious past, brought in external designers of note to execute special designs for the company, including Sir Terry Frost an eminent abstract painter, as well as Janice Tchalenko and Charlotte Mellis. Janice's studio pottery wares have been highly regarded for many years, having already found their way into most of the leading National museum collections, as well as many others abroad. Charlotte Mellis's work for Poole, 1997, features some very dramatic sweeping abstract curved designs in vivid colours, under the titles 'Blue Wash', 'Green Wash' and 'Blue/Yellow Wash'. One-off limited edition special productions have also come from outside with Lawrence McGowan creating a special plaque in celebration of the Antiques Roadshow twenty-first anniversary, whilst Julie Herring of Bournemouth University produced 'Creating a Brighter Future' in a limited edition of 250 plates of two sizes.

The most recent development at Poole has come from a joint effort between Alan Clarke and Anita Harris, working with Janice Tchalenko, this being the 'Living Glaze' technique. Owing much to the Delphis glaze effects of the 1960s, the revised and modernised approach display the innovative and unique new designs to dramatic effect. Allan Clarke's 'Eclipse' design is a perfect example of the evocative new technique. This design together with Clarke's design, 'Millennium', are limited edition, 1,999 for the former and 2,000 for the latter, but both designs are also made as more standard wares in three different sized dishes with an additional vase for the Millennium. The latest pieces of 'Living Glaze' wares have been commissioned by the Guild of Fine China & Glass Retailers, based in Manchester, with the Third Millennium dish (16.5 inches) being produced in a limited edition of 1,000, with four other 'Living Glaze' ten inch plates being produced exclusively for the Guild until March 2000 after which they will be available generally.

Janice Tchalenko is still very much an important part of the design team at Poole, although she treads a lonely road as a studio pottery and designer working within the ceramics industry, apparently pushed to the margins of studio pottery by her fellow potters. At least the management within Poole recognise not only the vitality of her work but also, and perhaps of greater significance, the encouragement and willingness Janice gives to her colleagues at Poole. The general public, it would appear, strongly support her as the new

'Living Glaze' designs are proving to be extremely successful, with demand exceeding the output. No doubt the popularity of this type of ware, along with others, will increase even further following the exhibition of the new designs, now including the work of Tony Morris, at the Richard Dennis Gallery in London.

In yet another interesting development Tony Morris, mentioned above, has been invited to return to Poole to design some one-off designs which is particular pertinent as Tony's original 1960s and 1970s designs have recently started to be eagerly sought after in auction rooms throughout the country and even via the Internet. Tony created a series of one-off dragonfly designs in 1999 all, with one exception on circular plaques, the other design for a set of four tiles, with one design also appearing to be based on a setting sun behind trees. The work of the Poole Studio must be seen in conjunction with that of the commercial tableware, ornamental ware and gift ware side of production, as more often than not ideas generated in one department are used in the other. Allan Clarke's skills and knowledge of the airbrush technique, combined with stencilling, have created some highly innovative and individual work, well as working in conjunction with Anita Harris to produce the distinctive 'Bluebell' and 'Fraiche' tableware designs, reflecting on the 1950s two-tone or Twintone wares. The entwined relationship between the two departments, reflecting that of the tile and commercial departments in earlier years, is a vital part of Poole Pottery, as is, and has always been, the frequent external input and influences of other fine arts, designers and the like.

As has been mentioned already, in previous decades under the Carter management, understanding the importance of keeping a balance in the wares being produced is vital, as is the need to react to and reflect changes in high street style and new fashions. Employing a new generation of young designers together with a deeper and more involved understanding of what various foreign and local markets require has enabled Poole Pottery, once again, to rank amongst the top British ceramic manufacturers. The importance of the direction and vision of Peter Mills, as managing director, should not be over looked. Nothing happens in any business without the support and commitment, whether overtly or by devolved responsibility of the management. In recent years, Poole Pottery having been steered back to the top of the ceramics business in the early 1990s, it has become apparent that the achievements of those years have spawned numerous rewards, high profile visits and exciting new commissions. At the end of the day it is only by displaying the products of the company in more and more places, whether the shop window of Bergdoff Goodman on Fifth Avenue, New York; Bloomindales on Third Avenue, New York City; David Jones in Australia; Harrods of Knightsbridge or at the trade show in Frankfurt or the NEC in Birmingham. Wherever the wares are shown only the wares can speak for themselves.

The sudden rise in the company's fortunes during the 1990s has been quite dramatic, to the point that today as I understand it, the company has out grown itself or rather its own buildings. The current position, as far as I can gather, is that the main production side of the pottery is about to move into new premises on a local industrial estate with some of the most up-to-date equipment that is currently available. Much of the current production site is either going to be sold and/or developed into a new shopping, leisure, marina and hotel complex. This with the exception of the current Poole showrooms, museum and tourist visitors centre which will largely remain as it is, possibly with some further modernisation and improvement.

As we usher in the new millennium, Poole Pottery would appear to be equipping itself to be around for at least another one hundred years, perhaps more.

Green lustre stone ware vase, designed by Owen Carter. 1900-1918. 6¼ ins. £200-£350/$330-$370.

Ruby lustre wall charger, designed by Owen Carter and dated 1903. 1900-18. 18 ins. £500-£800/$825-$1480.

Carter Tiles promotional model of a lion, circa 1905, modeller unknown. Inscribed around the base; Poole, Lustres, Mosaics, Terracotta, Faience, Carters Tiles (4¾ ins long). Green glaze. £100-£150/$165-$275.

An early Carter & Co lustre vase, c1908. £450-£650/$740-$1200.

Unglazed wares designed by James Radley Young, c1914. These wares are paler and unrefined compared to the later modified versions and were left with unturned bases. Left vase: £120-£180/$200-$335. Plate (13 ins) £200-£300/$330-$555. Two handled vase: £200-£350/$330-$645. Right £100-£150/$165-$275.

A selection of early tin-glazed wares, 1915-20, hand painted with simple decorative sprigs reflecting influences from Dutch tin-glazed wares at the same time establishing the body-type for the Poole Pottery. Left: £80-£120/$130-$220. Back vase (8½ ins high) £180-£220/$295-$405. Front £200-£300/$330-$555. Right £120-£180/$200-$335.

A tall tin-glazed earthenware vase (14½ ins), 1921-24. £350-£450/$575-$830.

Unglazed ware, 1925-34. Left: £80-£120/$130-$220; Large vase (13 ins), £400-£600/$660-$1110. Right £40-£60/$65-$110.

A selection of early tin-glazed wares, 1915-22, hand painted with simple foliate sprigs. The bowl at the front has a 'Made for Liberty' mark, £200-£250/$330-$460. Back vase (9¾ ins) £120-£180/ $200-$335. Right vase £200-£250/ $330-$460.

Left: an Erna Manners designed dish, 10½" diameter, 1921. £150-£250/$245-$460. Right: a John Adams plate design, 9" diameter c1924. £200-£250/ $330-$460.

A group of early tin-glazed earthenware based wares, 1921-24, mostly designed by Truda Adams after similar designs by James R Young. Left £150-£250/$245-$460. Back (14½ ins) £350-£450/$575-$830. Right back £120-£200/$200-$370. Front left £150-£250/$245-$460. Front middle £60-£90/$100-$165. Front right £80-£120/$130-$220.

A rare Joseph Roelants model of a mother and child, c1917, in a white tin-glazed covered white stoneware body. Several such figures were exhibited at the 1917 British Industries Fair, tile designs by Roelants also being shown at this fair (4¾ ins). £300-£600/$495-$1110.

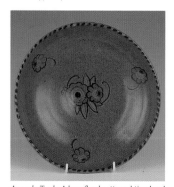

An early Truda Adams floral patterned tin-glazed dish (9⅜ ins), 1921-24, £250-£350/$410-$645.

A Truda Adams designed shallow bowl, 1924-27 (13½ ins diameter). £350-£500/$575-$925.

A rare Truda Adams designed dish with the Persian Bird pattern amongst flowering branches (12 ins diameter), late 1920s. This is, so far, the only known extant dish with the Persian bird pattern amongst flowering branches. £350-£450/$575-$830.

A Truda Adams designed red earthenware vase, 10½ inches high, c1924. £400-£600/$660-$1110.

A rare John Adams vase with Mondrianesque abstract design (9¾ ins), 1930s. £400-£650/$660-$1200.

The Bull. Designed by Harold and Phoebe Stabler, initially designed and modelled in 1914 and later made at Poole from 1922 to the 1930s (13½ ins high). £1600-£2500/$2640-$4625.

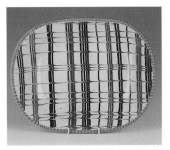

A combed slip trailed dish after a design by John Adams (14¾ ins, 1926-30. £200-£300/$330-$555.

Left: Truda Adams geometric hand painted design, 1927-34. £200-£300/$330-$555. Middle: a two handled vase with a bird on a branch designed by Truda Adams. £150-£250/$245-$460. Right: a two handled vase with a Truda Adams geometric design, after a design by James R Young, 1925-34, (6 ins high). £250-£400/$410-$740.

A Truda Adams decorated planter, 1920s. £300-£400/ $495-$740.

Left: a geometric patterned bowl, 1927-34, designed by Truda Adams. £120-£180/$200-$335. Front: Truda Carter designed vase (4 ins high), 1930-33. £80-£120/$130-$220. Back: John Adams designed splashed glaze pattern, 1930s. £200-£250/$330-$460. Right: Truda Carter patterned vase with a highly geometric and brightly coloured pattern, 1930s. £150-£250/$245-$460.

A Truda Adams designed pattern on a powder box and cover, 1925-32. £120-£180/$200-$335.

Left: a very rare bowl (currently the only one known to exist) decorated with a Truda Carter design of a parrot perched on a branch, 1934-37, (10¾ ins diameter). £400-£600/$660-$1110. Right: a Truda Carter 'Cocky Ollie Bird' design on a bowl, 1930-34. £250-£350/$410-$645.

A blue-bird decorated two-handled bowl designed by Truda Adams, 1930s, the shape designed by Harold Stabler (7 ins diam), 1925-26. £300-£500/$495-$925.

Left: a Truda Adams patterned biscuit box and cover, 1928-34, with two globular tulip-like flower heads. £220-£280/$365-$520. Front: a Waterbird decorated mug designed by Harold Stabler, 1922. £100-£150/$165-$275. Back: an early Carters Green glazed vase after designs by James Radley Young, 1920s. £120-£180/$200-$335. Right: a Truda Carter pattern adapted from an earlier James Radley Young design 1925-34. £120-£180/$200-$335.

A lavishly decorated Blue Bird design by Truda Adams (12"), late 1920s. £1400-£1800/$2310-$3330.

A rare Truda Adams design of a polychrome floral basket, the reverse with a triple flower group within an irregular chevron frame, late 1920s. £1000-£1400/$1650-$2590.

A John Adams leaping stag decorated plate (12½ ins diam), early 1920s. £400-£600/$660-$1110.

A rare large John Adams leaping stag decorated vase, (11 ins high) 1925-34. £800-£1200/$1320-$2220.

A large lavishly decorated leaping stag vase designed by John Adams (13 ins), late 1920s. £1800-£2200/$2970-$4070.

A Truda Adams charger with deer amongst foliage (15 ins), 1920s. £400-£700/$660-$1295.

A large Truda Adams Persian deer vase, the stag amongst polychrome flowers and foliage, (15 ins high) 1930s. £800-£1200/$1320-$2220.

Left: a Truda Carter designed vase, 1930s. £400-£600/$660-$1110. Front: a two-handled globular vase with a Truda Adams design of a bird amongst flowers. £300-£500/$495-$925. Right back: a tall vase with a Truda Adams design of a bird amongst flowers in a panel (9 ins). £300-£500/$495-$925. Right: a polychrome beaker vase with a Truda Carter floral design, 1930s. £120-£180/$200-$335.

A Truda Adams floral patterned vase, 1925-34 (10 ins high). £400-£700/$660-$1295.

A rare Truda Adams charger (11¾ ins) decorated with a stylised tree and exaggerated flower heads, 1928-34. £400-£600./$660-$1110

Left: a lavish boldly coloured Truda Carter designed vase with overlapping flowers and foliage, 1932 (9½ ins high). £1000-£1500/$1650-$2775. Centre: a Truda Carter leaping stag vase, 1930-34 (8¼ ins high). £600-£800/$990-$1480. Right: a rare abstract decorated vase designed by Truda Adams, 1928-1934. £800-£1000/$1320-$1850.

A very rare and lavishly decorated vase designed by Truda Adams, late 1920s (13 inches high). £2800-£3800/$4620-$7030.

A Truda Adams abstract patterned vase (7¼ ins), late 1920s, the shape designed by Harold Stabler. A similar vase and pattern were exhibited in the British Industries Fair, 1931, the piece fitted as a lamp base. £400-£700/$660-$1295

A Truda Carter trumpet shaped vase with a highly geometric pattern (9¾ ins), early 1930s. £600-£900/$990-$1665.

Four highly geometric patterned vases each designed by Truda Carter, early 1930s. Left: £500-£800/$825-$1480. Front: £300-£400/$495-$740. Back (8¼ ins) £200-£300/$330-$555. Right: £300-£450/$495-$830.

A abstract patterned dish designed by Truda Carter, with stylised tulips amongst scrolls and chevrons in a band c1930. £350-£500/$575-$925

An unusual boldly decorated abstract patterned small ginger jar and cover (7¾ins), 1930s, designed by Truda Carter. £1200-£1800/$1980-$3330.

Three highly abstract designs by Truda Carter. The two-handled vase on the left dating from about 1930, shows a typical experimental use of a two colour palette, £700-£900/$1155-$1665. Middle: early 1930s. £300-£400/$495-$740. Right: an unusual pattern dating from the early 1930s. £800-£1200/$1320-$2220.

Bell formed spill vase, with an abstract Truda Carter design, early 1930s. £100-£180/$165-$335.

A colourfully decorated Truda Adams stylised floral patterned vase, 1928-1934 (11 ins high). £600-£900/$990-$1665.

A large Truda Adams decorated stylised floral patterned vase (10 ins), 1928-34. £600-£800/$990-$1480.

The 'Leipzig Girl' charger, designed by Olive Bourne, 1926-27. Named after appearing in the 1927 Leipzig Exhibition of Industrial Art (17½ ins diam). £1200-£1800/$1980-$3330.

A later version of a 1926-27 design by Olive Bourne (10 ins), 1950s. £120-£180/$200-$335.

A large vase (8¼ ins) with an Olive Bourne portrait design dating from 1926-27. £1200-£1800/$2220-$3330.

A later version of an Olive Bourne portrait design (11 ins) dating from the 1926-27. Although later this is still a relatively rare piece and therefore has a value of between £400-£700/$660-$1295.

A rare and impressive two-handled vase designed by Truda Carter, hand painted with vertical panels of stylised over-lapping elongated foliage, 1930-34 (10¼ ins high). £1500-£2500/$2475-$4625.

A vase (8¼ ins) with a design by Truda Carter, 1930-34, handpainted with Persian stylised flower heads over chevron vertical columns. £3000-£4000/$4950-$7400.

A good two-handled vase (8½ ins) designed by Truda Carter, hand painted with panels of over-lapping elongated foliage, 1930-34. £700-£1000/$1155-$1850.

A good two-handled boldly patterned vase (7 ins) designed by Truda Carter, 1930-34, £800-£1200/$1320-$2220.

A Truda Adams patterned vase (11½ ins), 1926-34. £600-£900/$990-$1665.

A Truda Carter highly stylised foliate patterned vase (9¾ ins), 1930-34. £800-£1200/$1320-$2220.

A Truda Carter highly stylised foliate patterned vase (9¾ ins), 1930-34. £800-£1200/$1320-$2220.

A Truda Carter ginger jar and cover with a highly stylised design (7¼ ins), 1930-34. £800-£1200/$1320-$2220.

Left: a faceted vase with a scattered series of designs by Truda Carter on a coloured slip, 8 ins high, 1930-34. £700-£1000/$1155-$1850. Right: a two-handled vase with a stylised foliate design on a white slip designed by Truda Carter, 7 ins high, 1930-34. £700-£1000/$1155-$1850.

A tall Truda Carter cylindrical vase with a flared mouth (9¾ ins), 1930-34. £600-£900/$990-$1665.

A group of Truda Carter designed vases and a bowl, 1930-34. Front left: £150-£250/$245-$460. Back left (9 ins) £350-£450/$575-$830. Bowl: £300-£400/$495-$740. Right back: £220-£280/$365-$520.

A Truda Carter vase with a highly stylised foliate and geometric pattern (10½ ins), 1930-34. £800-£1200/$1320-$2220.

Two biscuit barrels and an unusual vase designed by Truda Carter, 1930-34. left (6 ins) £200-£300/$330-$555. Middle: £250-£350/$410-$645. Right: £200-£300/$330-$555.

A large Truda Carter vase decorated with highly stylised foliage (10¼ ins), 1930-34. £700-£1000/$1155-$1850.

Three highly stylised Truda Carter foliate designs with large stylised flowers amongst foliage, 1930-34. Left: £180-£220/$295-$405. Middle (11 ins) £400-£500/$660-$925. Right: £200-£300/$330-$555.

Three Truda Carter designed vases showing variations of the same pattern, 1930-34. Left: £200-£300/$330-$555. Middle (8 ins) £400-£500/$660-$925. Right £200-£300/$330-$555.

A large and impressive Truda Carter designed vase with stylised flowers amongst geometric motifs (14 ins), 1930-34. £2000-£2500/$3300-$4625.

A Truda Carter designed vase decorated with a broad band of stylised foliage, between wavy bands (10½ ins), 1930-34. £600-£800/$990-$1480.

A highly stylise and simplified version of the multi-bell formed flowers with lighting flash decoration on the boarder (8½ ins), 1930-34. £150-£250/$245-$460.

A fine highly stylised multi-bell formed Truda Carter pattern on a swelling cylindrical body (11½ ins), 1930-34. £800-£1200/$1320-$2220.

A rare large Truda Carter designed stylised floral pattern (12 ins), 1930-34. £1200-£1800/$1980-$3330.

An unusual octagonal sided bowl (4½ ins high) designed by John Adams, 1930s. £500-£700/$825-$1295.

A rare highly stylised almost abstract floral decorative pattern designed by Truda Carter (6¾ ins), 1930s. £600-£800/$990-$1480.

An usual Truda Carter designed with a simplified abstract cloud-like pattern in vertical sections (7 ins), 1930s. £300-£500/$495-$925.

A good Truda Carter designed vase (6¾ ins) with an over-lapping double lappet band, 1930s. £300-£400/$495-$740.

An abstract decorated Truda Carter designed vase (7 ins), 1930s. £300-£500/$495-$925.

A Truda Carter patterned candlestick with highly stylised flowers amongst chevron bands (9½ ins), 1930s. £200-£300/$330-$555.

A Truda Carter stylised floral vase, against a partial trellis ground (9¾ ins), 1930s. £700-£900/$1155-$1665.

Left: a Truda Carter designed animal plate, 1930s. £200-£350/$330-$645. Right: an abstract patterned dish (10¾ ins) designed by Truda Carter, 1930s. £300-£450/$495-$830.

A limited palette Truda Carter designed vase with stylised flowers (10½ ins), 1930-34. £500-£700/$825-$1295.

A rare Truda Carter designed vase (9¾ ins) with a strong abstract pattern, late 1930s. £1200-£1800/$1980-$3330.

Two interesting Truda Carter octagonal vases, 1930s, each decorated with same pattern in different colourways. Left (5¼ ins) £300-£400/$495-$740. Right: £300-£400/$495-$740. Middle: £200-£300/$330-$555.

A group of Truda Cater stylised floral designs, 1930s. Left back: £300-£500/$495-$925. Front left: £150-£250/$245-$460. Back right (8 ins) £350-£450/$575-$830. Front right £200-£300/$330-$555.

A two-handled Truda Carter design vase (9 ins) with a tinted ground, late 1930s. £400-£600/$660-$1110.

Three Truda Carter vases with pastel tinted grounds, c1934. Left (9 ins) £300-£400/$495-$740. Middle £120-£180/$200-$335. Right: £350-£450/$575-$830.

A lightly decorated vase (11¼ ins) designed by Truda Carter, with repeated berry and leaf motifs in vertical bands, 1950s. £350-£550/$575-$1015.

A Truda Carter stylised foliate decorated plate (13 ins), dated 1939, commissioned by W.T.Lamb & Sons to be given as Christmas presents £350-£450/$575-$830.

The reverse of dated plate, 1939.

A Truda Carter design vase (5 ins) with a highly stylised foliate and cloud pattern on a tinted ground, 1930s. £300-£500/$495-$925.

A faceted Truda Carter designed vase (8 ins) with stylised floral sprays on a tinted ground, 1930s. £300-£500/$495-$925.

A Truda Carter designed stylised floral plate (9½ ins dia) on a tinted ground, late 1930s. £500-£700/ $825-$1295.

A slightly tapering cylindrical vase (9 ins) decorated with a highly stylised foliate pattern in limited colours on a tinted ground, designed by Truda Carter, c1934. £400-£600/$660-$1110

Three Truda Carter designed vases showing some of the variety of colourways used during the mid 1930s period. Left: £300-£500/$495-$925. Middle (9 ins) £400-£600/$660-$1110. Right: £250-£450/$410-$830.

Primrose. An Arthur Bradbury designed wall plaque hand-painted after a design dating from the 1930s (15 ins). £500-£800/$825-$1480.

The Sea Adventure. An Arthur Bradbury designed wall plaque painted in 1951 after an original design dating from the 1930s (15 ins) . £500-£800/$825-$1480.

Reverse of Sea Adventure.

The Golden Hind. From a drawing by Margaret Holder (12½ ins), 1979. £300-£400/$495-$740.

Waterwitch. An Arthur Bradbury designed plate, handpainted in 1955 after an original design dating from the 1930s (11 ins). £300-£500/$495-$925.

Reverse of Waterwitch.

The Mayflower. Designed and painted by Ruth Pavely (12¼ ins), 1957. £300-£400/$495-$740.

A collection of candelabra designed by John Adams, initially designed in 1928-29, each modelled with grapes and vine leaves, with faceted arms and stand, raised on a slightly domed circular foot. Front left: £120-£180/$200-$335. Back left (11 ins) £250-£350/$410-$645.. Middle £180-£250/$295-$460. Right £80-£120/$130-$220.

Two large models of fish probably designed by John Adams, late 1930s, each decorated with sprayed Picotee glazes. Left (7½ ins) £150-£250/$245-$460. Right (8¼ ins) £150-£250/$245-$460.

A triple candelabra possibly designed by John Adams, late 1930s, with two birds in flight amongst stylised flowers and foliage, raised on a stepped rectangular base (11⅝ ins). £180-£280/$295-$520. Front: a small double candleholder, late 1930s. £25-£45/$40-$85.

A John Adams model of a leaping Springbok in the form of a book-end (8 ins), raised on a stepped rectangular base, c1930. £200-£400/$330-$740 for a single model.

A pierced octagonal tray with a bird in flight amongst flowering branches in sprayed Picotee glazes (12 ins long), late 1930s. £150-£250/$245-$460.

A collection of various shell designs by John Adams, late 1930s. Left: £15-£20/$25-$35. Back left: £25-£35/$40-$65. Front (10 ins long) £25-£40/$40-$75. Right back: £30-£50/$50-$80.

A Nursery Rhyme decorated plate (5 ins) designed by Dora Batty, used on nursery wares and toilet sets, 1921-22. £60-£80/$100-$150.

Left: a John Adams designed small bowl with a toilet set design of two owls, 1922-23. £100-£150/$165-$275. Middle: an Eileen McGrath 'Circus' decorated mug (4¼ ins), 1934-35. £100-£150/$165-$275. Right: a Harold Stabler 'Waterbirds' patterned mug after a design from about 1922. £100-£150/$165-$275.

Three items with a design from the Nursery Rhymes series by Dora Batty, 1921-22. Left: small beaker £60-£80/$100-$150. Bowl (13⅛ ins) £250-£350/$410-$645. Jug £250-£350/$410-$645.

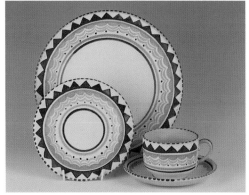

Two variations of an abstract geometric polychrome banded design, late 1920s early 1930s. Left: two handled vase £400-£650/$660-$1200. Middle: £200-£250/$330-$460. Right (9¾ ins) tinted glaze - £400-£650/$660-$1200.

Part of a tableware service designed by Truda Adams (plate 9¼ ins), late 1920s. £100-£150/$165-$275.

Mug from the Eileen McGrath Circus designs, (1950s). £100-£150/$165-$275.

Plate from the Elieem McGrath Circus designs (5 ins), 1934-35. £150-£250/$245-$460.

A Tall vase designed by Truda Carter with a wide band of highly stylised flowers, below ziggurat banding (11 ins), mid 1930s. £500-£800/$825-$1480.

A collection of egg cups dating from the 1920s. £10-£30/$15-$55 each.

Two jam pots and two small vessels after designs by Truda Adams, dating from the late 1920s and early 1930s. Left: £150-£250/$245-$460. Front: £50-£90/$80-$165. Back (5¼ ins) £150-£250/$245-$460. Right: £50-£90/$80-$165.

A Truda Carter designed vase (6½ ins), 1930-35. £120-£180/$200-$335. Centre: Sugar sifter with a design after Truda Carter mid 1930s. £30-£50/$50-$90. Right: Shallow bowl with a Truda Carter abstract pattern in a band. £80-£120/$130-$220

A bird design on a bowl by Truda Adams design, made specifically for Beale's of Bournemouth (11ins diameter). Late 1930s. £200-£300/$330-$555.

Honey box design by Harold Brownsword with the Little Red Riding Hood nursery ware design by Dora Batty (4¾ ins wide), c1934. £250-£350/$410-$645.

Stoneware seated model of a cat, c1934, decorated with a semi-matt black Zulu glaze, as it was known at the pottery, and is part of the Sylvan range. Modeller unknown, (8 ins high). £250-£450/$410-$830.

Two handle vase (9 ins) with a hand painted design probably decorated by Erna Manners with a design of berries and leaves, 1920-22. £350-£450/$575-$830.

Three Plane Ware vessels, 1930s, designed by John Adams. Left (5 ins) £100-£250/$165-$460. Middle: £80-£150/$130-$275. Right: £80-£120/$130-$220.

A collection of Everest Wares with angular forms and semi-matt white and pastel glazes, 1930s. Left: £120-£150/$200-$275. Back (6 ins) £180-£250/$295-$460. Front: £80-£120/$130-$220. Right: £120-£150/$200-$275.

Three vessels decorated with the Picotee Ware glazes developed by Leslie Elsden, 1930s. Back (11¾ ins) £150-£350/$245-$645. Front: £50-£80/$80-$150. Right: £120-£150/$200-$275.

Studland shaped coffee pot designed by Harold Stabler, c.1930 (6½ ins), with a Truda Carter floral design of the 1930s. £100-£150/$165-$275.

Three Sylvan Ware vessels dating from the mid 1930s showing the typical use of monochrome slightly mottled glaze effects on hand thrown and slip cast wares. Left (9¾ ins) £150-£250/$245-$460. Middle: £150-£250/$245-$460. Right: £150-£250/$245-$460.

Two slip-cast Plane wares, 1930s. Hand thrown with applied handles. Left (8¼ ins) £150-£250/$245-$460. Double handled bowl £200-£300/$330-$555.

Two hand-thrown vases, 1930s. Left: John Adams glazed vase (9¼ ins) £150-£250/$245-$460. Middle: Chinese blue glazed vase £250-£450/$410-$830. Right: Sylvan Ware vase £200-£300/$330-$555.

A special commission Wadington's bowl showing the four suits from a pack of card, 1950s (9¾ ins). £200-£300/$330-$555.

A 1951 Festival of Britain butter dish and cover. Left: £60-£120/$100-$220. Right (4⅛ ins) An invite to the 1998 book launch by Richard Dennis Publications. £40-£80/$65-$150.

Commemorative Coronation plate, 1953, Queen Elizabeth II (8½ ins). £60-£80/$100-$130.

Two hand thrown cylindrical vases by Jimmy Soper, early 1950s. Left (7¼ ins) £150-£200/$245-$370.. Right £120-£180/$200-$335.

Three Claude Smale and Guy Sydenham designed carafes designed c1951, with stylised Truda Carter floral designs, the Red Pippin design on the right. Left: (10 ins) £180-£300/$295-$555. Middle: £150-£250/$245-$460. Right: £180-£300/$295-$555.

Two Claude Smale and Guy Sydenham designed carafes, c.1951, and a vase possibly designed by John Adams, 1930s, each painted with repeated vertical lines by Alfred Read, from 1953-54. Left (10 ins) £150-£250/$245-$460. Middle: £80-£120/$130-$220. Right: £60-£80/$100-$150.

A Claude Smale and Guy Sydenham designed carafe, c1951, with a repeated wavy foliate design by Alfred Read (11¾ ins), from 1953-54. £200-£300/$330-$555.

Three Claude Smale and Guy Sydenham designed carafes, c.1951, decorated with alternate vertical lines of stars and lines of solid colour by Alfred Read, from 1954. Left (11¾ ins) £300-£500/$495-$925. Middle: £120-£150/$200-$275. Right: £300-£500/$495-$925.

Four graduated carafes designed by Claude Smale and Guy Sydenham, c1951, each with alternate vertical lines of stylised foliage and fronds designed by Alfred Read, from 1953. Left to right: £80-£120/$130-$220; £120-£150/$200-$275; £150-£200/$245-$370; £200-£350/$330-$645

Three hand thrown decorated vases with wide bands in bracken and purbeck colours with intertwined spirals, designed by Alfred Read, from 1954. Left (10½ ins) £150-£250/$245-$460. Middle: £80-£120/$130-$220. Right: £150-£250/$245-$460.

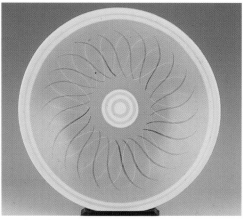

Large plate with intertwined spiral design on a purbeck ground by Alfred Read, from 1954 (13 ins). £150-£250/$245-$460.

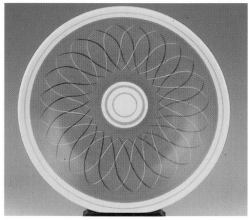

Large plate with intertwined spiral design on a bracken ground by Alfred Read, from 1954 (13 ins). £150-£250/$245-$460.

Three contemporary designed vessels by Alfred Read, 1953-54. Left (6¾ ins) £150-£300/$245-$555. Middle - £150-£300/$245-$555. Right: a unique trial piece - £200-£350/$330-$645.

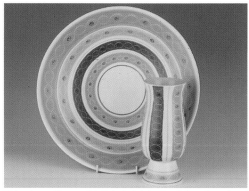

Plate and vase with narrow intertwined spirals forming circles on three coloured bands designed by Alfred Read, 1953-54. Left (13 ins dia) £150-£350/$245-$645. Right: £120-£180/$200-$335.

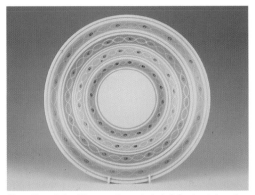

Plate with a variation of the narrow intertwined spirals forming circles on three coloured bands designed by Alfred Read (13 ins), 1953-54. £150-£350/$245-$645.

Two peanut thrown vases and another vase each with three vertical coloured bands containing intertwined spirals forming circles, designed by Alfred Read, 1953-54. Left (18 ins) £500-£800/$825-$1480. Middle: £150-£250/$245-$460. Right: £150-£250/$245-$460.

A peanut shaped vases, a tall bottle vase and another each with three vertical coloured bands containing intertwined spirals forming circles, designed by Alfred Read, 1953-54. Left: £150-£250/$245-$460. Middle: £150-£250/$245-$460. Right (15¾ ins) £300-£600/$495-$1110.

A group of Alfred Read designed wares, 1954, with repeated broken bracken coloured bands on thin parallel lines. Left: £100-£180/$165-$335. Middle: £180-£250/$295-$460. Middle right: £80-£120/$130-$220. Right: £180-£300/$295-$555.

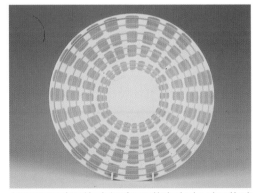

A contemporary plate with a design of repeated broken bracken coloured bands on thin parallel lines by Alfred Read (13 ins), 1954. £150-£350/$245-$645.

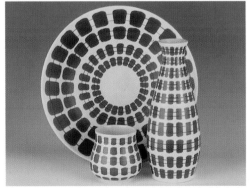

Three contemporary pieces with a colour variation, charcoal, of the broken repeated bands on thin parallel line designed by Alfred Read, 1954. Left: £100-£150/$165-$275; Plate (13 ins) £150-£350/$245-$645. Right: £200-£350/$330-$645.

A group of Alfred Read designed vases, 1954, each with repeated solid lime coloured horizontal bands over lines of rectangular motifs. Left: £120-£200/ $200-$370. Left middle (15½ ins) £300-£600/$495-$1110. Middle: £150-£250/$245-$460. Right middle: £200-£350/$330-$645. Right: £300-£600/ $495-$1110.

Two contemporary vessels with designs by Alfred Read, 1954, each with repeated solid lime coloured horizontal bands over lines of rectangular motifs. Left: £80-£120/$130-$220. Right (14½ ins) £300-£600/$495-$1110.

A group of contemporary vases each with a design of alternating vertical intertwined spirals in charcoal and terra cotta by Alfred Read, 1954. Left (10½ ins): £250-£450/$410-$830. Front left: £120-£200/$200-$370. Middle: £200-£350/$330-$645. Front right: £80-£120/$130-$220. Right: £200-£300/$330-$555.

A group of contemporary vases each with a design by Alfred Read, 1954, of alternating vertical intertwined spirals in charcoal and terracotta. Left: £200-£350/$330-$645. Front: £120-£200/$200-$370. Back: £200-£400/$330-$740. Middle right: £100-£150/$165-$275. Front right: £80-£120/$130-$220. Back right (10¾ ins) £200-£350/$330-$645.

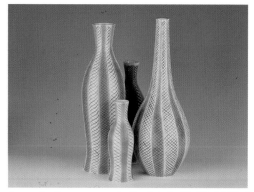

A group of contemporary vases each with a design by Alfred Read, 1954, of alternating vertical intertwined spirals in charcoal and terracotta. Left: £300-£600/$495-$1110. Front: £120-£200/$200-$370. Back: £150-£250/$245-$460. Right (15¾ ins) £300-£600/$495-$1110.

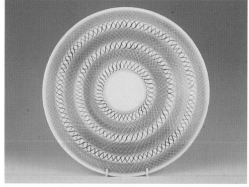

A contemporary plate with a design of alternating vertical intertwined spirals in charcoal and terra cotta by Alfred Read (13 ins), 1954. £150-£350/$245-$645.

Two vases each with an alternating vertical intertwined spirals in charcoal and lime designed by Alfred Read, 1954. Left: £200-£350/$330-$645. Right (15¼ ins) £300-£600/$495-$1110.

A mixture of Alfred Read designs for contemporary pieces, 1953/4. Back left: £180-£280/$295-$520. Back middle: £150-£250/$245-$460. Back right (12⅝ ins) £180-£280/$295-$520. Front left: £100-£180/$165-$335. Front middle: £80-£150/$130-$275. Front right: £120-£200/$200-$370.

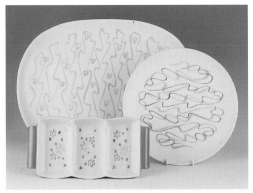

Three Alfred Read designs, 1953. A 'Constellation' triple serving dish. £30-£50/$50-$90. A large 'Ripple' serving dish in purbeck and lemon (16¼ ins long). £20-£50/$35-$90. An 'Ariadne' plate in terracotta and glacier blue. £40-£60/$65-$110.

A group of Alfred Read designs, 1953-54. Ripple jam pot. £20-£35/$35-$65. Ariadne plate. £20-£30/$35-$55. Ariadne cup and saucer. £10-£20/$15-$35. Ripple plate. £10-£20/$15-$35.

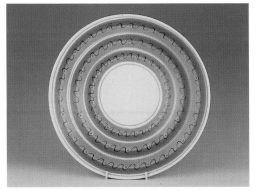

A Ruth Pavely designed plate, 1954, with repeated wavy line and dot motif in bands on alternating terracotta and turquoise solid coloured bands (13 ins). £150-£350/$245-$645.

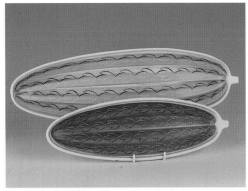

Two cucumber shaped dishes with repeated lines of outlined leaves on two colour bands designed by Ruth Pavely, 1954. Top (16⅛ ins long) £35-£55/$55-$65. Bottom: £25-£45/$40-$85.

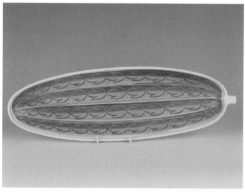

A cucumber shaped dish with a Ruth Pavely design of stylised leaves in a line on two colour bands, 1954. £25-£45/$40-$85.

A Ruth Pavely designed bowl with repeated two colour bands and leaf motifs in outline over the bands, 1954 (13⅞ ins). £150-£350/$245-$645.

A group of Alfred Read and Guy Sydenham designed monochrome glazed hand thrown vases and slip-cast freeform wares, 1954-57. Back left, ice green vase, £100-£200/$165-$370. Back middle, Sky Blue vase £50-£80/$80-$150. Back right freeform Magnolia White vase (14¼ ins) £100-£250/$165-$460. Front Black Panther freeform bowl £30-£60/$50-$110.

A group of Alfred Read and Guy Sydenham designed monochrome glazed hand thrown vases and slip-cast freeform wares, 1954-57. Back left: freeform Black Panther vase (14¼ ins) £150-£250/$245-$460. Back middle: Sky Blue bottle vase £150-£250/$245-$460. Back right: Lime Green vase £80-£120/$130-$220. Front: Magnolia White freeform vase £150-£250/$245-$460.

A group of Alfred Read and Guy Sydenham designed monochrome glazed hand thrown vases and slip-cast freeform wares, 1954-57. Back left, Black Panther freeform vase (8 ins) £100-£150/$165-$275. Back right, Red Indian freeform vase £150-£250/$245-$460. Front left, Lime Green vase £50-£80/$80-$150. Front right, hand thrown Ice Green vase £40-£60/$65-$110.

A hand thrown Alfred Read and Guy Sydenham designed vase with a Black Panther glaze (10¼ ins). £60-£80/$100-$150.

An unusual and rare hand thrown irregular bowl signed by Guy Sydenham, painted 19.9.57 (6½ ins high). £350-£650/$575-$1200.

Rare Alfred Read designed vases, 1953/5, probable produced as one-off studio wares for exhibitions and display. Left (7⅞ ins) £150-£250/$245-$460. Middle: £200-£300/$330-$555. Right: £150-£250/$245-$460

A large Poole Pottery display wall plaque designed by Ann Read, 1956, (14 ins long). £350-£650/$575-$1200.

Two Ann Read designed display plates (13 ins diameter), early 1950s. Left, entitled 'Snow Goose' £150-£250/$245-$460. Right, entitled 'Reflections' £150-£250/$245-$460.

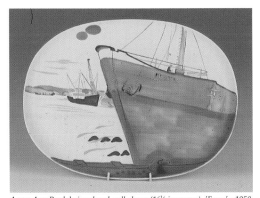

A rare Ann Read designed oval wall plaque (16¼ ins across), 'Freya', c1958. One of only three numbered pieces. This is No: 1 and is signed by Ann Read. £600-£800/$990-$1480.

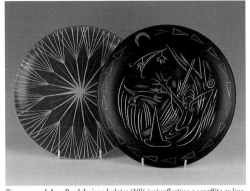

Two unusual Ann Read designed plates (10½ ins) reflecting a sgraffito or lino-cut style of white lines on a black ground, 1955-56. Left: £100-£150/$165-$275. Right: £150-£250/$245-$460.

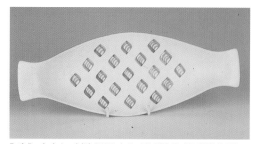

Ruth Pavely designed dish (12⅜ ins), Ravioli, 1956-57. £25-£45/$40-$85.

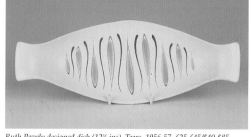

Ruth Pavely designed dish (12⅜ ins), Tears, 1956-57. £25-£45/$40-$85.

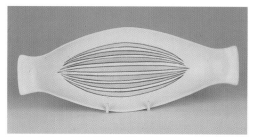

Ruth Pavely designed dish (12⅜ ins), Slits, 1956-57. £25-£45/$40-$85.

Ann Read designed dish (12⅜ ins), Basket, 1956-57. £25-£45/$40-$85.

Ruth Pavely designed dish (12⅜ ins), Tears, 1956-57. £25-£45/$40-$85.

Ruth Pavely designed dish (12⅜ ins), Tears, 1956-57. £25-£45/$40-$85.

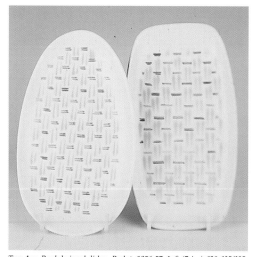

Two Ann Read designed dishes, Basket, 1956-57. Left (7 ins) £20-£35/$35-$65. Right £20-£35/$35-$65.

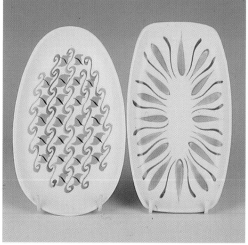

Two Ruth Pavely designed dishes, 1956-57, Scroll (left, 7 ins) £20-£35/$35-$65. Tears (right) £20-£35/$35-$65.

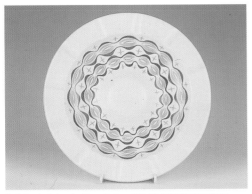

Ruth Pavely designed ashtray, Onions, 1956-57. £80-£120/$130-$220.

Three Ruth Pavely vases, 1956-57. Left, Peanut shaped vase with one off trial pattern £300-£600/$495-$1110. Middle, freeform Burst vase (14¼ ins) £300-£600/$495-$1110. Right, freeform Horizontal Rope £300-£600/$495-$1110.

Left, Basket pattern vase designed by Ann Read £300-£600/$495-$1110. Middle, Harlequin designed by Ruth Pavely £300-£600/$495-$1110. Right, Bamboo designed by Ann Read (14¼ ins) £300-£600/$495-$1110.

Two Ruth Pavely patterned vases and basket pattern vase by Ann Read, 1956-57. Left, Totem (14¼ ins) £300-£600/$495-$1110. Middle, Basket: £300-£600/$495-$1110. Right, One off trial pattern £300-£600/$495-$1110.

Two Ruth Pavely patterned vases and Basket pattern by Ann Read, 1956-57. Left: Scroll (8 ins) £300-£600/$495-$1110. Middle: Totem: £180-£280/$295-$520. Right: Basket, £150-£250/$245-$460.

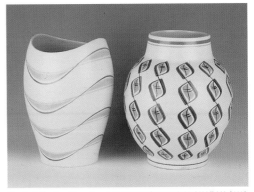

Two Ruth Pavely patterned vases, 1956-57. Left: Loops £400-£600/$660-$1110. Right: Harlequin (10 ins) £400-£600/$660-$1110.

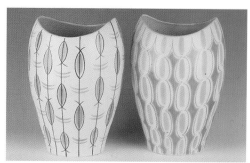

A freeform vase, 1956-57 by Ruth Pavely, left, Totem (10 ins) £400-£600/$660-$1110 and Bamboo by Ann Read, right, £400-£600/$660-$1110.

A Ruth Pavely patterned vase (9 ins high), 1956-57. Scroll pattern, £300-£600/$495-$1110.

Two Ruth Pavely patterned vases, 1956-57. Left. Harlequin;. Right, Ravioli (9 ins) each £300-£600/$495-$1110.

A Ruth Pavely patterned freeform vase (7 ins high), 1956-57. Left Loops. Right, an Ann Read Bamboo patterned vase. Each £300-£600/$495-$1110.

Three Ruth Pavely patterned vases, 1956-57. Left: Scroll £200-£300/$330-$555. Middle, Loops (14¼ ins) £300-£600/$495-$1110. Right: Burst £300-£600/$495-$1110.

Three Ruth Pavely patterned vases, 1956-57. Left: Scroll (9½ ins) £180-£250/$295-$460. Middle: Butterflies, £180-£250/$295-$460. Right: Horizontal Rope £180-£250/$295-$460.

A collection of small free form vases (4 ins) with Ruth Pavely designs and basket designed by Ann Read, including: Loops, Tadpoles, Stars, Totem, Bamboo and Bursts. Each £20-£45/$35-$85.

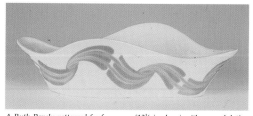

A Ruth Pavely patterned freeform vase (13¾ ins long) with an undulating ribbon trial pattern, 1956-57. £200-£300/$330-$555.

A collection of Bkohara wares designed by Robert Jefferson, c1964. Left, vase in black and blue glaze (8 ins high) £30-£60/$50-$110. Front, kitchen jar £20-£40/$35-$75. Back: preserve jar £20-£40/$35-$75. Right: preserve jar £20-£40/$35-$75.

Two spice jars and a storage jar designed by Robert Jefferson with a green diamond pattern, c1963. Two spice jars £15-£25/$25-$45. Storage jar £20-£35/$35-$65.

Left a Delphis carved vase, early 1970s £60-£100/$100-$185. Middle modern Picotee glaze (15½ ins) £60-£100/$100-$185. Right 1960s Delphis £60-£100/$100-$185.

An early Delphis Studio plaque (16 ins), mid 1960s. £250-£400/$410-$740.

Three early Delphis Studio ware pieces, mid to late 1960s. Back (14¼ ins) £150-£300/$245-$555. Middle: £75-£150/$125-$275. Front: £10-£25/$15-$45.

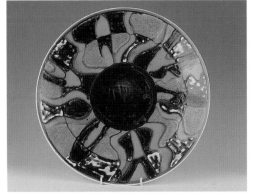

An early Delphis Studio plaque (14⅛ ins), mid to late 1960s. £300-£400/$495-$740.

Four early Delphis Studio dishes, mid to late 1960s. Back left (8 ins) £75-£200/$125-$370. Back right £10-£35/$15-$65. Front left £10-£35/$15-$65. Front right £10-£35/$15-$65.

Four early Delphis Studio dishes, mid to late 1960s. Back left (8 ins) £75-£200/$125-$370. Back right £75-£200/$125-$370. Front left £10-£35/$15-$65. Front right £10-£35/$15-$20.

Three early Delphis Studio dishes, mid to late 1960s. Left (8 ins) £75-£200/$125-$370. Middle £75-£200/$125-$370. Right £10-£35/$15-$65.

Three early Delphis Studio dishes, mid to late 1960s. Left (8 ins) £75-£200/$125-$370. Middle £75-£200/$125-$370. Right £10-£35/$15-$65.

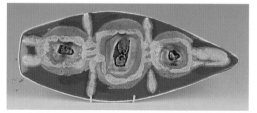

An early Delphis shield shaped dish, mid to late 1960s, (17 ins long). £35-£65/$55-$120.

A rare Delphis Studio wall plaque by Pamela Bevans, c1970, depicting a pelican (16 ins). £300-£500/$495-$925.

Five small Delphis Studio ware dishes (5 ins), late 1960s. Each between £10-£35/$15-$65.

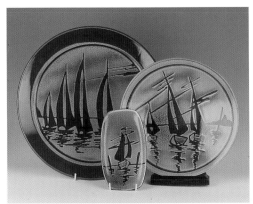

Three Aegean ware pieces after a design by Leslie Eldsen, early 1970s, using the silhouette technique. Back circular plate (13¾ ins) £30-£60/$50-$110. Front dish £15-£20/$25-$35. Right: £20-£40/$35-$75.

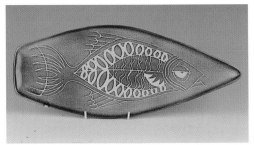

An Aegean shield shaped dish, 1970s (17 ins long). £40-£60/$65-$110.

An Aegean shield shaped dish, 1970s (17 inches long). £20-£40/$35-$75.

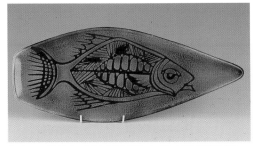

An Aegean shield shaped dish, 1970s (17 inches long). £20-£40/$35-$75.

Three Aegean ware vases, 1970s. Left: £100-£200/$165-$370. Middle: £80-£150/$130-$275. Right: £80-£150/$130-$275.

Three Aegean ware vases, 1970s. Left: £80-£150/$130-$275. Middle: £80-£150/$130-$275. Right: £60-£100/$100-$185.

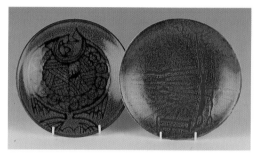

Two Aegean decorated plates, early 1970s. Left, fish plate £20-£40/$35-$75. Right, landscape plate £20-£40/$35-$75.

An Aegean ware circular plate after a design by Leslie Elsden, early 1970s. £20-£40/$35-$75. A Sea Crest cruet set designed by Toni Morris and Guy Sydenham, late 1960s. £20-£40/$35-$75.

Three Aegean ware dishes, 1970s. Left: £10-£25/$15-$45. Middle: £10-£25/$15-$45. Right: £10-£25/$15-$45.

An Olympus range vase (9¼ ins) with a design by Ros Sommerfelt, late 1970s. £80-£120/$130-$220. An Studio red earthenware hand thrown vase, mid 1960s. £200-£300/$330-$555. An Atlantis Studio vase of gourd form by Guy Sydenham, mid 1960s. £200-£400/$330-$740.

A collection of Atlantis red earthenware hand thrown and carved gourd-like forms, 1970s, after designs by Guy Sydenham. Left back (8 ins) £150-£350/$245-$645. Middle back: £150-£350/$245-$645.. Front left: £150-£350/$245-$645. Middle: £150-£350/$245-$645. Front middle: £150-£350/$245-$645. Back right: £150-£350/$245-$645. Right: £150-£350/$245-$645.

A Sienna vase designed by Toni Morris and Jacqueline Leonard, 1978, with a resist pattern under spray colours on a white earthenware body (9 ins). £60-£80/$100-$150.

A rare Atlantis Guy Sydenham designed vase (12 ins), 1970s, with monkey faces amongst palm leaves carved around the neck under a wide flared rim of the hand thrown body. £1500-£2000/$2475-$3700.

A Commemorative plate 'The Queen's Silver Jubilee, 1952-1977,' depicting a lion and a unicorn in the stained glass technique designed by Toni Morris. Limited edition of 250, 12½ ins. £150-£250/$245-$460.

A collection of Beardsley decorated wares, from 1979, designed by Ros Sommerfelt. Left back, a rare hand-painted table lamp by S Pottinger (10 ins) £200-£400/$330-$740. Left front £30-£50/$50-$90. Right front £30-£50/$50-$90. Right back, ginger jar and cover £100-£150/$165-$275.

A collection of Beardsley decorated wares, from 1979, designed by Ros Sommerfelt. Left: £30-£50/$50-$90. Front left £30-£50/$50-$90. Front right £30-£50/$50-$90. Right pair candlesticks £40-£60/$65-$110. Back (8 ins) £120-£150/$200-$275.

Two Charlotte Mellis Poole Studio Collection dishes, 1997. Left, Blue Wash; Right, Green Wash. Each £80-£150/$130-$275.

A Sir Terry Frost designed dish, Arizona Blue, 1996 (16¼ ins). £350-£450/$575-$830.

Trial plate by Ros Sommerfelt, 1990s (13¾ ins). £150-£250/$245-$460.

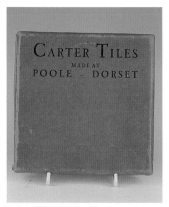

A Carter Tiles promotional box for two terracotta floor tiles. £20-£30/$35-$55.

A Poole Pottery promotional tile, 1950s. Such a tile can be seen illustrated as part of the 1950s exhibition display stands at the Tea Centre, Regents Street, London. £25-£35/$40-$65.

A rare early Carter & Co peacock tile with coloured slip trailing and hand-painting (6 ins square), c1900. £120-£150/$200-$275.

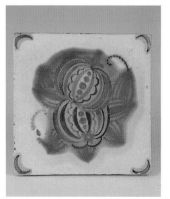

A rare early Carter & Co fruits and leaves tile with coloured slip trailing and hand painting 6 ins square), c1900. £60-£80/$100-$150.

A rare Carter, Stabler & Adams floral hand painted tile, possibly after a design by Truda Adams (6 ins square), 1920s. £30-£40/$50-$75.

A rare Carter, Stabler & Adams fruit and foliage hand painted tile, possibly after a design by Truda Adams (6 ins square), 1920s. £30-£40/$50-$75.

An early Joseph Roelants designed rectangular hand painted tile, 1917-20, depicting Dutch peasants at work from the 'Dutch Scenes' Series. £80-£120/$130-$220.

An early Joseph Roelants designed hand painted tile, 1917-20, depicting Dutch peasant from the 'Dutch Scenes' series. £35-£50/$55-$90.

An early Joseph Roelants designed hand painted tile, 1917-20, depicting Dutch peasants from the 'Dutch Scenes' series. £35-£50/$55-$65.

An early Joseph Roelants designed handpainted tile, 1917-20, depicting Dutch peasants from the 'Dutch Scenes' Series. £35-£50/$55-$90.

A later Joseph Roelants tile design from the 'Dutch Scenes' series, polychrome silk-screen printed (6 ins square), 1950s. £25-£45/$40-$85.

Later Joseph Roelants tile design from the 'Dutch Scenes' series, polychrome silk-screen print. 1950s. £25-£45/$40-$85.

Later Joseph Roelants tile design from the 'Dutch Scenes' series, polychrome silk-screen print. 1950s. £25-£45/$40-$85.

Later Joseph Roelants tile design from the 'Dutch Scenes' series, polychrome silk-screen print. 1950s. £25-£45/$40-$85.

Later Joseph Roelants tile design from the 'Dutch Scenes' series, polychrome silk-screen print. 1950s. £25-£45/$40-$85.

One of a group of tiles designed by Harold Stabler for the London Passenger Transport Board to used on at certain underground train stations, 1938-39. Moulded in the form of a Swan with a crown around its neck (6 ins square). £80-£120/$130-$220.

One of a group of tiles designed by Harold Stabler for the London Passenger Transport Board to used on at certain underground train stations, 1938-39. Moulded with the dome of St Paul's and the letters St P (6 ins square). £80-£120/$130-$220.

An Edward Bawden design from his 'Chase' series, 1920s, (6 ins square). £30-£50/$50-$90.

Later Joseph Roelants designed tile from the 'Boat' series, 1950s, polychrome hand-painted. £20-£40/ $35-$75.

Later Joseph Roelants designed tile from the 'Boat' series, 1950s, polychrome hand-painted. £20-£40/ $35-$75.

Later Joseph Roelants designed tile from the 'Boat' series, 1950s, polychrome hand-painted. £20-£40/ $35-$75.

Later Joseph Roelants designed tile from the 'Boat' series, 1950s, polychrome hand-painted. £20-£40/ $35-$75.

Joseph Roelants designed tile from the 'Boat' series, 1950s, polychrome silk-screen printed. £20-£40/ $35-$75.

Joseph Roelants designed tile from the 'Boat' series, 1950s, polychrome silk-screen printed. £20-£40/ $35-$75.

An Edward Bawden design from his 'Sporting' series, 1920s (5 ins square). £30-£50/$50-$90.

An Edward Bawden design from his 'Sporting' series, 1920s, (5 ins square). £30-£50/$50-$90.

An Edward Bawden design from his 'Sporting' series, 1920s, (6 ins square). £30-£50/$50-$90.

An Edward Bawden design from his 'Chase' series, 1920s, (6 ins square). £30-£50/$50-$90.

A Cecil Aldin design from a series of 'Dog' tiles, 1930s to 1950s. £35-£50/$55-$90.

Fish tile design in surrounding Dutch style. Dated 1933. £30-£40/$50-$75.

A Harold Stabler designed tile from the 'Water Bird' series, 1920s to 1950s. £25-£45/$40-$85.

Harold Stabler designed tiles from the 'Water Bird' series, 1920s to 1950s. £25-£45/$40-$85.

Harold Stabler designed tiles from the 'Water Bird' series, 1920s to 1950s. £25-£45/$40-$85.

Chickens, an early handmade tile with canted edges and no mark. It was designed by Truda Adams. £25-£45/$40-$85.

Dora M. Batty designs from the 'Nursery Toys' series, 1920s to 1950s. £25-£45/$40-$85.

Dora M. Batty designs from the 'Nursery Toys' series, 1920s to 1950s. £25-£45/$40-$85.

Dora M. Batty designs from the 'Nursery Toys' series, 1920s to 1950s. £25-£45/$40-$85.

Designs by Dora M. Batty from the 'Nursery Rhymes' series, 1920s to 1950s. £25-£45/$40-$85.

Designs by Dora M. Batty from the 'Nursery Rhymes' series, 1920s to 1950s. £25-£45/$40-$85.

An Alfred B Read tile design from the 'Play Box' series, 1950s and 60s. £35-£50/$55-$90.

An Alfred B Read tile design from the 'Play Box' series, 1950s and 60s. £35-£50/$55-$90.

An Alfred B Read tile design from the 'Play Box' series, 1950s and 60s. £35-£50/$55-$90.

Polychrome stencilled 'Farmyard' tile designs by E E Strickland, 1920s to 1950s. £35-£55/$55-$100.

Polychrome stencilled 'Farmyard' tile designs by E E Strickland, 1920s to 1950s. £35-£55/$55-$100.

Polychrome stencilled 'Farmyard' tile designs by E E Strickland, 1920s to 1950s. £35-£55/$55-$100.

Polychrome stencilled 'Farmyard' tile designs by E E Strickland, 1920s to 1950s. £35-£55/$55-$100.

Polychrome stencilled 'Farmyard' tile designs by E E Strickland, 1920s to 1950s. £35-£55/$55-$100.

Polychrome stencilled 'Farmyard' tile designs by E E Strickland, 1920s to 1950s. £35-£55/$55-$100.

Polychrome stencilled 'Farmyard' tile designs by E E Strickland, 1920s to 1950s. £35-£55/$55-$100.

Polychrome stencilled 'Farmyard' tile designs by E E Strickland, 1920s to 1950s. £35-£55/$55-$100.

Polychrome stencilled 'Farmyard' tile designs by E E Strickland, 1920s to 1950s. £35-£55/$55-$100.

Polychrome stencilled 'Farmyard' tile designs by E E Strickland, 1920s to 1950s. £35-£55/$55-$100.

Susan Williams Ellis designs from the "Sea" series, 1950s to 1960s. £20-£25/$35-$45.

Susan Williams Ellis designs from the "Sea" series, 1950s to 1960s. £20-£25/$35-$45.

Three stencilled Reginald Till designs from the 'English Countryside' series, 1950s and 1960s. Each £20-£35/$35-$65.

Three Phyllis Butler designed tiles from the 'Field Grasses' series, 1950s and 1960s. Each £15-£25/$25-$45.

Two kitchen tile designs, designers unknown, from two such series, 1960s. Each £10-£15/$15-$25.

Above: Six white glazed hand tube lined tile designs on a matte black terracotta unglazed tiles. Designer unknown (4 ins square), 1950s. Each £20-£35/$35-$65.

Right: Four polychrome hand painted tile designs showing medieval subjects, 1950s and 1960s. Each £25-£45/$40-$100.

A collection of early Carter & Co glazed wares, 1900-25.
Top: left £150-£200/$245-$370.
Top middle: £220-£320/$365-$590.
Top middle right: £80-£120/$130-$220.
Top right: £120-£180/$200-$335.
Middle left £200-£300/$330-$555.
Middle centre: £150-£200/$245-$370.
Middle right: £180-£220/$295-$405.
Right: £150-£200/$245-$370.
Bottom: left £200-£300/$330-$555.
Bottom middle: £200-£300/$330-$555.
Bottom right: £250-£350/$410-$645

A collection of unglazed ware designed by Truda Adams after designs by James Radley Young, 1921 to the early 1930s. Top: left £150-£250/$245-$460. Left mid £80-£120/$130-$220. Middle: £60-£90/$100-$165. Mid right: £80-£120/$130-$220. Right: £150-£250/$245-$460. Middle: left £200-£300/$330-$555. Back: £200-£300/$330-$555. Front: £120-£180/$200-$335. Right: £250-£350/$410-$645. Bottom: back left £250-£350/$410-$645. Back mid: £200-£300/$330-$555. Back right: £300-£400/$495-$740. Front: left £150-£250/$245-$460. Front right: £150-£250/$245-$460.

A collection of jam pots and vessels with Truda Adams/Carter, 1920s and 1930s, together with a Picotee Ware jam pot (bottom centre left), 1930s. Each between £40-£80/$65-$150.

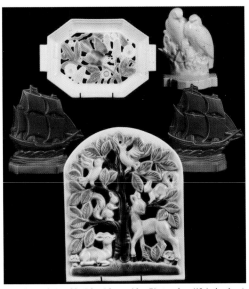

Pierced tray designed by John Adams with a Picotee glaze (12 inches long), 1940s. £150-£250/$245-$460. A Love Birds bookend designed by John Adams, 1930s. £350-£450/$575-$830. A pair of ship bookends after a design by Harold Stabler, 1930s. £600-£800/$990-$1480. A pierced wall plaque designed by Lily Markus, 1940s, in a Picotee glaze. £200-£400/$330-$740.

A collection of John Adams designed wall mounts. A sailing yacht £60-£90/$100-$165. Three flying ducks £200-£300/$330-$555. Set of three graduated sailing yachts £300-£400/$495-$740. A seagull £80-£120/$130-$220. A sailing boat (large) £120-£180/$200-$335. Three flying blue birds £200-£300/$330-$555.

Three graduates flying seagulls £250-£350/$410-$645. Two deer £100-£150/$165-$275. A circular brooch £80-£150/$130-$275. A shield shaped pendant £50-£90/$80-$165.

A large Truda Carter design floral wall plaque (15 inches diameter) £300-£500/$495-$925. A Large Ship wall plaque after a design by Arthur Bradley, entitled General Wolfe, late 1930s, (15 inches diameter) £600-£900/$990-$1665.

A Queen Elizabeth II Coronation Commemorative vase, 1953. £200-£300/$330-$555. A Poole presentation vase, Poole Swimming Club, 1930s. £180-£280/$295-$520. A Poole Swimming Club Jubilee Gala plate, 1935. £180-£220/$295-$405.

An Ionian circular plate, mid 1970s. £180-£280/$295-$520. An Aegean charger depicting a street scene £300-£500/$495-$925. A tall carved Delphis vase, late 1960s £350-£450/$575-$830. A small carved Delphis vase £120-£180/$200-$335. A small Delphis vase £60-£80/$100-$150. A small Delphis vase £80-£120/$130-$220. Three moulded trays in the form of a knife £40-£60/$65-$110 each.

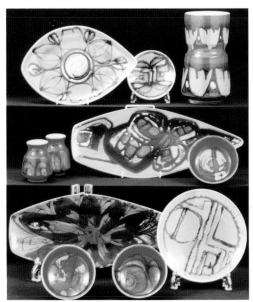

A collection of later mainly standard Delphis ware, 1970 to 1979. Top: left dish £30-£60/$50-$100. Middle: small dish 15-£25/$25-$45. Right: vase £60-£90/$100-$165. Middle: two vases £40-£80/$65-$150. Long dish £100-£200/$165-$370. Right: small dish 15-£25/$25-$45. Bottom: left back long dish £100-£200/$165-$370. Front two dishes 15-£25/$25-$45 each. Right: £50-£90/$80-$165.

A collection of later standard Delphis wares, 1969-79. Top: £150-£250/$245-$460. Middle: left £100-£150/$165-$275. Back: £120-£180/$200-$335. Right: £40-£80/$65-$150. Bottom: left £200-£300/$330-$555. Back: £200-£300/$330-$555. Right: £150-£250/$245-$460

A collection of Aegean wares, 1970-79. Top plate £60-£80/$100-$150. Middle Corfe Castle dish £80-£120/$130-$220. Left ship plate £80-£150/$130-$275. Middle Snowflake plate £25-£45/$40-$85. Right 'Harry Paye' plate designed by Toni Morris £150-£250/$245-$460. Right Knight on horseback £120-£150/$200-$275. Bottom vase 15-£25/$25-$45.

A collection of Aegean wares, 1969/79. Top: left £40-£80/$65-$150. Middle landscape plate £80-£150/$130-$275. Right pair £80-£120/$130-$220. Middle: left galleon plate £120-£200/$200-$370. Middle: vase £50-£90/$80-$165. Right: fish plate £60-£100/$100-$185. Bottom: left vase £60-£100/$100-$185. Middle: 'Harry Paye' plate £180-£280/$295-$520. Small vase £30-£50/$50-$90. Right: vase £80-£140/$130-$260.

A collection of mainly Atlantis wares, 1972-77. Top: left small vase £40-
£60/$65-$110. Vase £50-£100/$80-$185. Right: slip trailed plate designed by
John Adams, late 1920s £120-£220/$200-$405. Middle: left lamp vase £180-
£250/$15-$460. Small vase £80-£120/$130-$220. Circular plaque £120-£220/
$200-$405. Right: carved vase £100-£200/$165-$370. Bottom: carved vase £80-
£120/$130-$220. Plate £30-£80/$50-$150. Front: small carved vase £30-£50/
$50-$95. Tall vase £50-£90/$80-$165. Left: carved vase £40-£90/$65-$165.

A collection of Atlantis wares mostly designed by Guy Sydenham, 1972-77,
and a wall plaque. Top: left dish £50-£90/$80-$165. Middle: New Stoneware
coffee pot, 1967, £50-£90/$80-$165. Right: fish dish £40-£80/$65-$150. Middle:
left speckle glazed vase £120-£220/$200-$405. Middle carved vase £120-
£180/$200-$335. Right dish £50-£90/$80-$165. Bottom: incised plaque of Corfe
Caste £60-£100/$100-$185. Front: left dish £40-£60/$65-$110. Right green
speckled and white dish £60-£90/$100-$165. Front: right £30-£50/$50-$90.

An Atlantis carved beer keg and mugs, 1970s. £200-£400/330-$740.

A collection of Barbara Linley Adams stonewares, introduced from 1972. Top:
small duck £20-£40/$35-$75. Plate £15-£25/$25-$45. Model of a wren £20-
£40/$35-$75. Seated dog £40-£70/$65-$130. Middle: small plate of an elephant
from the Wildlife Collection, 1982-84, (5 ins) £10-£20/$15-$35. Model of a
Hedgehog £20-£50/$35-$95. Model of a duck £150-£300/$245-$555. Bottom:
model of a goose £180-£300/$295-$555. Model of an owl £50-£80/$80-$150.

A gilt decorated black vase by Alan White, 1980s. Burnished gold on a matte black panther glaze (8½ ins). £60-£90/$100-$165.

Part of a set of Medieval Calendar plates designed by Toni Morris, limited edition of 1000 of each, 1972-75. Each between £150-£350/$245-$645. Middle: left A Cathedral plate, 'Christ on The Cross', designed by Toni Morris in a limited edition of 1000, 1973. £150-£350/$245-$645. Middle: right A commemorative wall plaque, 'The Saint George', 1977-78, designed by Toni Morris. Limited edition of 1000. £150-£350/$245-$645.

A Delphis Studio plate, early to mid 1960s (sold through Sotheby's Chester). Because this is quite likely to have been designed and painted by Tony Morris, compared to known examples and archive documentation this will have value of between £1500-£1800/$2475-$3330 even though it is only 8 inches in diameter.

A large impressive Delphis Studio dish, early 1960s, with a painted monogram for Tony Morris. At 16 3/4 inches in diameter this is certainly one of the largest dishes of its type. This dish was sold in Sotheby's Chester auction rooms in about 1987/88 for £462/$760. Should this particular dish appear on the market again it would almost certainly sell for between £3000-£6000/$4950-$11,100. Not a bad investment in just over ten years.

A large impressive Delphis Studio dish, early 1960s, with a painted monogram for Tony Morris. This abstract decorated dish is typical of the most sought after early Delphis which with the added weight of the Morris monogram would certainly mean a price of between £1800-£2800/$2970-$5180. This dish was also sold through the Sotheby's Chester auction rooms, along with two small plates (see latter illustrations) for £396/$650.

A Delphis Studio plate, 1960s, 8 inches diameter (sold in Sotheby's Chester). Typical of much of the early Studio Delphis wares this piece is not marked with a monogram which affects the price range, as does the size. £1200-£1500/$1980-$2775.

103

Egg Baker oven-to-tableware in celadon green, designed by Robert Jefferson, 1960s. Notice the packaging also probably designed by Roben. £30-£40/$50-$75.

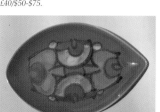

A two-handled red earthenware vase, early 1930s, decorated with a Truda Carter design (6½ ins high). £600-£800/$990-$1480..

by Jean Cockram with a two headed bird, a crescent in between, the top of each wing painted with a horse's head and the base of the tail with the head of a bull. The base marked Pembrok (14½ ins high). £800-£1200/$1320-$2320.

A Delphis dish decorated in standardised colours, 1970s, (12 ins long). £20-£30/$35-$55.

A large wall plaque, 'Sugar for the Bird', designed by Olive Bourne, 1920s. £100-£150/$165-$275.

A standard Delphis circular dish, 1970s (12 ins diameter). £20-£30/$35-$55.

A tall Delphis vase designed by Angela Wyburgh, 1968-69, with irregular impressions or dimples around the neck. (15¾ inches high). £350-£450/ $575-$830.

Three small standard Delphis dishes, 1970s (the largest 3 ins). £20-£30/$35-$55.

Price and Pattern Guide

The following price lists are to be regarded as 'rough' estimated guidelines. The estimated prices are the sort of pricing to be found on wares at an auction house level and therefore what might be considered middle level market prices. All estimated prices are for pieces in 'perfect' condition. The prices indicated may also, in some instances such as the Delphis and Aegean wares, refer to an average price as two identically shaped pieces with seemingly very similar patterns may have variably values depending on the designer/paintress/painter. There are inevitably going to be very many factors to take into account when you are assessing the price level of an item, such as condition, size, effectiveness of the decoration (Meaning the success or not of the decoration of a particular shape), the paintress/painter, etc. Equally you will find that the seller will have used similar judgements when deciding on a price that they would like to obtain for certain pieces, sometimes dependent on how much they want to sell it, how quickly they want to turn over their stock, etc. At the end of the day, how much you really want a certain piece or how much you think a piece is worth is entirely up to you.

Where there are no prices this is either because such wares very rarely appear on the market and therefore estimating values is somewhat redundant as it value will depend on the depth of the buyer's pockets/and or the desirability of the item. Other pieces without estimates may be due to the fact that they are still in production, in which case refer to the Pottery for current retail prices, or have been made in the last ten years or so and therefore usually, although not always, have values close to their retail value. Limited Edition pieces or wares that were only in production for a limited time may well attract various prices.

Sculptures and Figures

Advertising Lion. Modelled lying on a stepped rectangular base, a shield below its chin. Designer unknown. Used as advertising model between 1905 and the late 1920s. £100-£150/$165-$290.

Joseph (Jozef) Roelants

Belgian Peasant Folk Modelled by Joseph (Jozef) Roelants, circa 1917. White stoneware body and white tin glaze (8¾ins). £400-£800/$660-$1560.

Mother and Child Modelled by Joseph (Jozef) Roelants, marked 'Carter's Poole, 1916, Belgium'. White tin glaze over a white stoneware body (5¾ins). £300-£600/$495-$1170.

Candleholder Modelled by Joseph (Jozef) Roelants, as a red glazed figure dressed in long robes carrying a basket, formed into a candle sconce, raised on an unglazed circular domed stepped base, red stoneware body, marked 'Carters Poole', 'J. Roelants' on the side. (6¼ins). £400-£800/$660-$1560.

'The Flight from Louvain' Modelled by Joseph Roelants, one of numerous figures and groups exhibited at 1917 British Industries Fair (whereabouts unknown). £600-£1000/$990-$1950.

Harold & Phoebe Stabler

These figures were in the main made and modelled by Harold and Phoebe Stabler using a buff coloured stoneware clay prior to the couples association with the Poole Pottery in 1921. Many models were later made as slip cast figures at the Poole Pottery. Other works designed by the Stablers and produced at Poole also exist, such as the polychrome roundel probably emblematic of Spring exhibited at the British Industries Fair in 1921, the faience panels modelled in 1924, exhibited at the Wembley Empire Exhibition and later installed in the mortuary chapel, Mary Abbots, Kensington Infirmary. (the prices given are for Poole Pottery models).

Picardy Peasants Designed by Phoebe Stabler, 1911. Two figures seated on stepped rectangular bases (c.10¼ins). Later made at Poole from 1922 through to the 1930s. £250-£450/$410-$875.

Lavender Woman Designed by Phoebe Stabler, 1911. Seated woman holding a baby in her arms. Later made at Poole from 1922 through to the 1930s. £200-£400/$330-$780.

The Bull Designed by Harold and Phoebe Stabler, 1914. Later made at Poole between 1922 and the early 1930s (13ins). £1600-£2500/$2640-$4875.

The Piping Fawn Roundel designed by Phoebe Stabler, 1914, (plain) (15ins). Later made in plain and coloured versions at Poole, 1920 to 1930s. £800-£1000/$1320-$1950.

Piping Boy Designed by Phoebe Stabler, 1914-18 (14¾ins). Later made at Poole from early 1920s through to the 1930s. £500-£800/$825-$1560.

Shy Designed by Phoebe Stabler, 1914-18. £600-£900/$990-$1755.

Harpy Eagle Designed by Harold Stabler, 1916 (26ins). Introduced at Poole from the mid 1920s through to the 1930s. £500-£800/$825-$1560.

Buster Boy Designed by Phoebe Stabler, 1916. Introduced at Poole from the early 1920s. £350-£550/$575-$1070.

Buster Girl Designed by Phoebe Stabler, 1916. Introduced at Poole from the early 1920s. £350-£550/$575-$1070.

Bath Towel Two figures designed by Phoebe Stabler, Introduced at Poole from about 1922. £250-£350/$410-$680.

Fighting Cock Designed by Harold Stabler, 1923-24 (7½ins). Later made at Poole. £250-£400/$410-$780.

The Galleon Designed by Harold Stabler, circa 1925. This was to become synonymous with of the Poole Pottery. Made of red earthenware and at 20 inches high this should not be confused with the many later versions. £600-£1100/$990-$2145.

Spring Flowers Wall Medallion Designed by Harold Stabler, circa 1921. Decorated in Della Robbia style primary colours (14½ins). £600-£900/$990-$1755.

Summer Flowers Wall Medallion Designed by Harold Stabler, circa 1921. Decorated in Della Robbia style primary colours. £600-£900/$990-$1755.

Bird on Stump Designed by Harold Stabler whilst at the Poole Pottery, 1931 (6ins). £400-£600/$660-$1170.

St George Designed by Harold and Pheobe Stabler, 1922. Part of a commission for the Rugby School War Memorial. £1500-£3000/$2475-$5850.

The Goat Designed by Harold Stabler, mid 1920s (16ins). (Bronze metal versions of this model and its companion, The Bear, signed and dated 1928, 14⅛ inches high, are also known to exist). £350-£500/$575-$975.

The Bear Designed by Harold Stabler, mid 1920s (16ins). £350-£500/$575-$975.

Rabbit Designed by Harold Stabler, circa 1930. Vellum white glaze. £250-£350/$410-$680.

Eagle Designed by Harold Stabler, circa 1930. Vellum white glaze (7¼ins). £500-£800/$825-$1560.

Other artists

Elegant Figures – **Katherine**, **Elizabeth**, **Abigail**, **Eleanor**, **Victoria** and **Lillie**. Designed by John Bromley, made in white earthenware from 1980-81 and then produced in bone china from 1982 (10ins). £60-£90/$100-$175.

General – Book-ends and/or wall mounted ornaments

Love birds Designed by John Adams, late 1920s, celadon stoneware (see later version). £250-£450/$410-$875.

Ship Designed by Harold Stabler, modelled by Harry Brown, 1926 (10¾ins). £350-£500/$575-$975.

Ship Book-end, smaller version. £250-£350/$410-$680.

Springbok Book-end, designed by John Adams. £300-£500/$495-$975.

Basket of Flowers Designed by John Adams, 1930-31 (7ins). £300-£500/$495-$975.

Three Monkeys Designed by Hugh Llewellyn, 1922-23, buff stoneware (7¼ins). Later produced as a terracotta stoneware slip cast model. £300-£500/$495-$975.

Model of a Knight Designed by Harold Brownsword, 1928-30, stoneware, (8ins). £400-£600/$660-$1170.

Model of an Elephant Designed by Harold Brownsword, 1930, stoneware. These were later remodelled in about 1935 in earthenware. £250-£350/$410-$680.

Carter, Stabler and Adams blue glazed vase designs by John Adams and the Goat and the Bear book end models by Harold Stabler. Studio Yearbook, 1927.

Ornaments

Love Birds Modelled by Harry Brown, after a design by John Adams, 1935. Decorated using a Picotee glaze, earthenware body. This has an oval base as opposed to the shaped and faceted rectangular base of the original design. £350-£450/$575-$875.

Love Birds lamp base This is almost the same model as the Harry Brown version above, with the addition of a column in the form of a tree trunk, and the base as further detailing. The overall model is very crisp in design and can be covered a monochrome glaze. £400-£500/$660-$975.

Zulu cats Seated grey stoneware models of cats in a semi-matt black glaze, designer and modeller unknown, circa 1934, (8ins high). £250-£450/$410-$875.

Yachts

Racing Yacht Probably designed by John Adams, 1937-38. Two-tone colours. (15½ins). £120-£160/$200-$310. (10ins). £80-£120/$130-$235. (6¼ins). £50-£70/$80-$135. (4¼ins). £30-£50/$50-$95.

The Egeria Schooner. (As above, also made for wall mounting). £180-£260/$295-$505.

Wall vases

Flared Floral with scroll sides, 1930s, (24½ins high). £25-£45/$40-$85. (20 ins high). £20-£35/$35-$70.

Double pocket scallop outer bowl, 1930s, (8¼ins). £40-£60/$65-$115.

Elongated Floral with scroll sides (very like two above only narrower), 1930s, (12¼ins). £45-£60/$75-$115. (9 ins). £30-£45/$50-$85. (6¼ins). £20-£30/$35-$60.

Star shape 1930s, (7 ins). £40-£60/$65-$115.

Elongated scalloped body, with fan-shaped sides, 1930s, (20 ins high). £45-£60/$75-$115. (8⅝ ins). £35-£45/$55-$85. (6⅝ ins). £25-£35/$40-$70. (5 ins). £35-£45/$55-$85.

Birds

Ducks. Set of three wall mounted flying ducks, designed by John Adams, 1936-39. Pictoee glaze effects. (largest 11¾ins). £200-£300/$330-$585.

Seagulls Set of three wall mounted flying seagulls, designed by John Adams, 1936-39. Pictoee glaze effects. (largest 10½ins). £250-£350/$410-$680.

Blue Birds Set of three flying bluebirds, designed by John Adams, 1936-39. Pictoee glaze effects. (largest 5 ins). £200-£300/$330-$585.

Love Birds Wall mounted ornament, designed by John Adams, 1936-39. Pictoee glaze effects. (4ins). £350-£450/$575-$875.

Wall Mounted Heads

Alsatian Modelled by Harry Brown, 1930s, (4½ins). £20-£30/$35-$60.

Red Setter Modelled by Harry Brown, 1930s, (4ins). £20-£30/$35-$60.

Terrier Modelled by Harry Brown, 1930s, (4ins). £20-£30/$35-$60.

Greyhound Modelled by Harry Brown, 1930s, (4ins). £20-£30/$35-$60.

Bush Buck Head Designed by C.J. Astley Maberly, modelled by Harry Brown. 1950s. £30-£40/$50-$80.

Springbok Head Designed by C.J. Astley Maberly, modelled by Harry Brown. 1950s. £30-£40/$50-$80.

Lion Head Designed by C.J. Astley Maberly, modelled by Harold Brownsword. 1950s. £40-£80/$65-$155.

Leopard Head Designed by C.J. Astley Maberly, modelled by Harold Brownsword. 1950s. £40-£80/$65-$155.

Candleabra

Cherub Designed by Harold Brownsword, modelled holding a cornucopia of flowers, 1928-30. £80-£150/$130-$290.

Berry and Leaf Designed by John Adams, single branch candelabra, 1928-29 (7ins). £80-£120/$130-$235.

Berry and Leaf Designed by John Adams, triple branch candelabra, circa 1930 (8½ins). £180-£250/$295-$485.

Berry and Leaf Designed by John Adams, two branch candelabra, 1947-49. £120-£180/$200-$350.

Berry and Leaf Designed by John Adams, four branch candelabra, 1947-49. £250-£350/$410-$680.

Bird and Floral Possibly designed by John Adams, pierced two branch candelabra, 1933-37. £180-£220/$295-$430.

Single small spiral Candlestick, in Picotee glaze, late 1930s. £20-£30/$35-$60.

Miscellaneous

Pierced tray Octagonal handled tray depicting a bird in flight amongst flowers and foliage, 1930s, (12ins long). Decorated in Picotee glazes. £150-£250/$245-$485.

Pierced faience wall panel A leaping deer amongst foliage within a frame of pierced oriental style square tiles, probably designed by John Adams, 1932. £500-£800/$825-$1560.

Pierced animal wall panel Birds and squirrels in a tree with two bucks at the base, decorated in Picotee colours, designed by Lily Markus (12½ins). £200-£400/$330-$780.

Pierced faience wall panel Depicting bunches of grapes, foliage amongst repeated scrolls, designed by Reginald Till for the Carters stand at the 1927 Ideal Home Exhibition. Subsequently relocated into John Adams house at Broadstone. £400-£700/$660-$1365.

Shell moulded bowls and dishes – Produced in two tone colours between the 1930s to the 1950s.

Nautilus – Large, £40-£60/$65-$115. Medium, £25-£35/$40-$70. Small, £15-£20/$25-$40.

Winkle – Large, £30-£50/$50-$95. Medium, £25-£35/$40-$70. Small, £15-£20/$25-$40.

Scallop – Large, £25-£35/$40-$70. Small, £15-£20/$25-$40.

Conch – Large, £25-£40/$40-$80. Medium, £15-£25/$25-$50.

Rounded Shell – £20-£30/$35-$60.

Ashtray – Rowing Boat 1930s, two tone glaze. £20-£30/$35-$60.

Figural octagonal red stoneware, designed by Harold Brownsword, 1928-29. £60-£100/$100-$195.

Plates – **Octagonal embossed dessert plate** with a foliate border, 1930s. £60-£80/$100-$155.

Circular leaf and berry plate possibly embossed, 1930s. Two sizes. £60-£80/$100-$155.

Brooches Various Truda Carter designs were adapted for small, octagonal, oval and circular brooches, the designs including flowers, birds amongst flowers some of the brooches being pierced or moulded. These were made between 1939 and the 1950s. £60-£220/$100-$430.

Terrier head (1940-53). £20-£40/$35-$80.

Stylised Fish (1990). £20-£40/$35-$80.

Fish Models

Tall Fish Possibly designed by John Adams, 1930s. Pictoee glaze effects. (15ins). £150-£250/$245-$485.

Tall Fish Possibly designed by John Adams, 1930s. Pictoee glaze effects. (8¼ins). £120-£250/$200-$485.

Tall Fish Mounted on black rectangular stand. Possibly designed by John Adams, 1930s. Sylvan glaze effects. (17ins). £200-£400/$330-$780.

Long Fish Possibly designed by John Adams, 1930s. Pictoee glaze effects. (7½ins). £150-£250/$245-$485.

Small Fish Possibly designed by John Adams, 1930s. Pictoee glaze effects. (4ins). £40-£80/$65-$155.

Animals

Stylized Rabbit Designer and modeller unknown, made in two sizes, 1930s. £40-£60/$65-$115.

Airedale Dog Designed by John Adams, 1937-38. £30-£60/$50-$115.

Stylized Horses Designed by John Adams, two sizes, mid 1930s. £30-£60/$50-$115.

Model of a Bird Probably designed by John Adams, 1930s. £20-£40/$35-$80.

Seated Lamb Designed by Marjorie Drawbell, late 1940s. £70-£100/$115-$195.

New Forest Colt Designed by Marjorie Drawbell, late 1940s. £80-£120/$130-$235.

Bear Cub Designed by Marjorie Drawbell, late 1940s. This is one of six bear and bear cub designs from the late 1940s. These models can also be found in experimental glazes. £100-£200/$165-$390.

Rabbit Designed by Marjorie Drawbell, head turned to the left, late 1940s. £60-£100/$100-$195.

Gazelle Designed by Marjorie Drawbell, two sizes, (both illustrated in the *Decorative Art Studio Yearbook*, 1949) late 1940s. £80-£120/$130-$235.

Dolphin brooch Designed by Robert Jefferson, 1967-present. £50-£90/$80-$175.

Dolphin model Designed by Robert Jefferson, modelled by Tony Morris, small, 1967-present. £100-£150/$165-$290.

Dolphin model Designed by Robert Jefferson, modelled by Tony Morris, large, 1969-present. £100-£150/$165-$290.

Dolphin model Designed by Robert Jefferson, modelled by Bert Baggaley, medium, 1979-present. £80-£120/$130-$235.

Double Dolphin Designed and modelled by Tony Morris, large, 1987-present. £120-£150/$200-$290.

Double Dolphin Designed and modelled by Tony Morris, small, 1988-present. £60-£90/$100-$175.

Dolphin Tray Designed and modelled by Tony Morris, 1967-80. £40-£80/$65-$155.

Between 1975 and 1979 Tony Morris designed and modelled seven other similar sized trays including studies of; a penguin, fish, deer, seagull, squirrel an owl and a zebra. The latter appears not to be mentioned in the records.

Penguin Designed and modelled by Tony Morris, small, 1975-80. £20-£40/$35-$80.

Penguin Designed and modelled by Tony Morris, large, 1975-80. £30-£60/$50-$115.

Seal Designed and modelled by Tony Morris, 1976-96. £20-£40/$35-$80.

Squirrel Designed and modelled by Tony Morris, 1976-78. £20-£30/$35-$60.

Otter Designed and modelled by Tony Morris, 1976-96. £20-£30/$35-$60.

Seahorse brooch Designed and modelled by Tony Morris, 1979-82. £30-£50/$50-$95.

Whale Designed and modelled by Tony Morris, 1980-81. £30-£50/$50-$95.

Whale Designed and modelled by Tony Morris, second version, 1991-93. £20-£40/$35-$80.

Trout Designed and modelled by Tony Morris, 1981-82. £30-£50/$50-$95.

Trout Designed and modelled by Tony Morris, second version, 1995-present. £30-£50/$50-$95.

Alligator Designed and modelled by Tony Morris, 1981. £20-£40/$35-$80.

Alligator Designed and modelled by Tony Morris, second version, 1991. £20-£40/$35-$80.

Old English Sheepdog Designed and modelled by Bert Baggaley, 1981. £20-£30/$35-$60.

Scottish Terrier Designed and modelled by Bert Baggaley, 1981. £20-£30/$35-$60.

Afghan Hound Designed and modelled by Bert Baggaley, 1981. £20-£30/$35-$60.

Dachshund Designed and modelled by Bert Baggaley, 1981. £20-£30/$35-$60.

Yorkshire Terrier Designed and modelled by Bert Baggaley, 1981. £20-£30/$35-$60.

West Highland Terrier Designed and modelled by Bert Baggaley, 1981. £20-£30/$35-$60.

Cat Designed by Elaine Williamson and modelled by Alan Pepper, large, 1987-present. £30-£50/$50-$95.

Cat Designed by Elaine Williamson and modelled by Alan Pepper, small, 1987-present. £20-£40/$35-$80.

Duck Designed and modelled by Claire Heath, 1995-present. £15-£20/$25-$40.

Leaping Salmon Designed and Modelled by Claire Heath, 1995-present. £20-£50/$35-$95.

Cats Designed by the Ceramic Undertones Craft Centre, Poole, in buff stoneware, in the manner of Barbara Linley Adams, 1996. Includes; a large cat seated £20-£40/$35-$80; a large cat lying £20-£40/$35-$80; two kittens cleaning themselves £10-£20/$15-$40 and two kittens asleep £10-£20/$15-$40.

Springbok Reworked version of earlier model, issued in blue, green or beige, 1998. £80-£120/$130-$235.

Elephant Reworked version of earlier model, issued in blue, green or beige, 1998. £80-£120/$130-$235.

Bear Reworked version of earlier model, issued in blue, green or beige, 1998. £350-£500/$575-$975.

Galleon Reworked version of earlier model, issued in blue or polychrome, 1998. £600-£1100/$990-$2145.

Barbara Linley Adams 1972-83

During the eleven years that Barbara was associated with the Poole Pottery she modelled over 100 hundred animals and birds, the first being a Wren on a branch and varying in size from a few inches to about 15 inches. All the models were initially made in stoneware, a few being released in limited editions of 1,000 others made specifically for commission and after 1990, the first polychrome coloured versions appeared which are still being made.

From 1979, some of the models were produced in earthenware and between 1985 and 1986 a series of birds and a few animals were made in bone china.

Over the years several series of embossed and/or incised plates and single plates were also designed by Barbara Linley Adams, issued mostly in limited editions, all 8¼ins diameter, including:

Stoneware Animals:

Wren on Branch – 1972-74. £20-£40/$35-$80.

Wren on Apple – 1972-89. £20-£40/$35-$80.

Mouse on Apple – 1972-89. £20-£40/$35-$80.

Canada Goose – Limited edition 500. 1973-78. £50-£100/$80-$195.

Barred Owl – 1973-78. £60-£90/$100-$175.

Mallard Ducklng – 1973-78. £20-£40/$35-$80.

Mallard – Limited edition 1000. 1973-84. £50-£100/$80-$195.

Chickadee on pine cone – 1974-89. £20-£40/$35-$80.

Quail – 1974-81. £40-£60/$65-$115.

Pair of Sandpipers – Limited edition 1000. 1974-82. £80-£120/$130-$235.

Pair of Grouse – Limited edition 1000. 1974-82. £80-£120/$130-$235.

Thrush – 1975-83. £20-£40/$35-$80.

Little Owl – 1975-89. £30-£50/$50-$95.

Toad – 1975-77. £10-£20/$15-$40.

Mouse crouching – 1975-78. £10-£20/$15-$40.

Mouse sitting – 1975-78. £10-£20/$15-$40.

Mouse standing – 1975-7. £10-£20/$15-$40.

Dormouse awake – 1975-78. £10-£20/$15-$40.

Dormouse asleep – 1975-78. £10-£20/$15-$40.

Rabbit sitting – 1975-78. £15-£30/$25-$60.

Rabbit preening – 1975-78. £15-£30/$25-$60.

Rabbit washing – 1975-78. £15-£30/$25-$60.

Rabbit standing – 1975-78. £15-£30/$25-$60.

Merlin – 1977-89. £40-£60/$65-$115.

Fawn – 1977-84. £800-£1000/$1320-$1950.

Goldcrest – 1977-89. £20-£40/$35-$80.

Squirrel – 1977-82. £30-£50/$50-$95.

Cat – 1978-82. £40-£60/$65-$115.

Baby Owl – 1979-89. £20-£40/$35-$80.

Robin on flowerpot – 1979-89. £30-£50/$50-$95.

Tortoise – 1979-89. £20-£30/$35-$60.

Seal – 1979-82. £20-£30/$35-$60.

Small Fawn – 1979-89. £30-£50/$50-$95.

Blue Tit – 1980-89. £30-£50/$50-$95.

Hedgehog – 1980-89. £15-£30/$25-$60.

Otter – 1980-82. £30-£50/$50-$95.

Sparrow – 1980-84. £15-£30/$25-$60.

Fox paperweight – 1980-81. £20-£30/$35-$60.

Nuthatch – 1981-89. £30-£50/$50-$95.

Pony – 1981-83. £40-£60/$65-$115.

Robin on brick – 1981-89. £30-£50/$50-$95.

Wren on shoe – 1981-89. £30-£50/$50-$95.

Pair of Badgers – 1981-89. £50-£80/$80-$155.

Harvest Mouse – 1981-89. £10-£20/$15-$40.

Guinea Pig – 1984-89. £15-£25/$25-$50.

Fox – 1985-89. £30-£50/$50-$95.

Hound – 1985-89. £20-£30/$35-$60.

Vole – 1985-89. £20-£40/$35-$80.

Stoat – 1987-89. £20-£40/$35-$80.

Puppy on slipper – 1988-89. £30-£50/$50-$95.

Kookaburra – 1984-?. £30-£50/$50-$95.

Puffin – 1974-?. £30-£50/$50-$95.

Miscellaneous wares:

Mouse lamp base – 1982-83. £20-£40/$35-$80.

Bird lamp base – 1982-83. £400-£600/$660-$1170.

Owl & Mice lamp base – 1985-89. £80-£100/$130-$195.

Owl Carving – 1988. £60-£90/$100-$175.

Heron Carving – 1988. £60-£90/$100-$175.

Pony Heads – Shetland, Welsh Mountain, Exmoor, New Forest. 1980-81. £20-£40/$35-$80.

Decoy ducks – Each on oval bases; Pintail, Mallard, Great Crested Grebe, Teal, Tufted duck, Canada Goose. 1982. £60-£90/$100-$175 each.

The Four Seasons (quatrefoil wall plaques) (9ins x 8ins). 1983-89. £60-£90/$100-$175.

Limited Edition Plates:

British Birds – Limited to 5,000. Wren, Robin, Blue tit, Swallow (only produced up to 1981), Blackbird, Thrush (8¼ins). 1978-83. £20-£50/$35-$95.

North American Birds – Limited to 5,000. Mallard, Heron, Horned Owl, Bald Eagle (8¼ins). 1978-82. £20-£50/$35-$95.

Game Birds – Limited to 5,000. Pheasant, Red Grouse, Woodcock, Blackcock (8¼ins). 1982-84. £20-£50/$35-$95.

Mouse Plates – Mice eating blackberries (1982 only), mouse and butterfly, mouse eating nut, mouse and snail, harvest mice, mouse chasing leaves (1982 only). 1982-88. (5ins diameter.). £10-£20/$15-$40.

New Forest – Limited to 5,000. Rabbits, Foal, Deer, Fox (5ins). 1983-88. £10-£20/$15-$40.

Birds – Limited to 5,000. Baby Robin, Wren, Goldcrest, Owls (5ins). 1982-88. £10-£20/$15-$40.

Cats – Limited to 5,000. Cat and dragon fly, cat asleep, cat and wool, cat and butterfly (5ins). 1983-88. £250-£450/$410-$875.

Dogs – Limited to 5,000. Dachshund, Labrador, Beagle, Poodle (5ins). 1983-88. £10-£20/$15-$40.

Wild Animals – Limited to 5,000. Baby elephant, baby giraffe, lion cub, zebra foal (5ins). 1984-88. £10-£20/$15-$40.

Mouse – Limited to 5,000. Mouse and butterfly, mouse eating nut, mouse and snail, Harvest mouse (5ins). 1983-88. £10-£20/$15-$40.

Seal plate – Limited to 7,500, for the World Wildlife Fund (8¼ins). 1979-82. £20-£50/$35-$95.

Christmas plates: (all 8¼ins).

1978 **Santa's Helpers** – Limited to 10,000. £100-£200/$165-$390.

1979 **Three Wise Men** – Limited to 10,000. £100-£200/$165-$390.

1980 **Temptation** – Limited to 10,000. £100-£200/$165-$390.

1981 **Christmas Carol** – Limited to 5000. £100-£200/$165-$390.

1982 **Waiting for Santa** – Limited to 5000. £100-£200/$165-$390.

1983 **Playmates** – Limited to 5000. £100-£200/$165-$390.

1984 **Expectations** – Limited to 5000. £100-£200/$165-$390.

1985 **Carol Singers** – Limited to 5000. £100-£200/$165-$390.

1986 **Away in a Manger** – Limited to 10,000. £100-£200/$165-$390.

Mother's Day plates: (8¼ins.)

1979 **Tenderness** – Limited to 10,000. £80-£180/$130-$350.

1980 **Devotion** – Limited to 10,000. £80-£180/$130-$350.

1981 **For You** – Limited to 5000. £80-£180/$130-$350.

1982 **Family Frolics** – Limited to 5000. £80-£180/$130-$350.

1983 **Patience** – Limited to 5000. £80-£180/$130-$350.

1984 **Puppy Love** – Limited to 5000. £80-£180/$130-$350.

Other Designers

Map plates, designed by Tony Morris between 1963 and 1978. The initial idea for these largely commission-based wares developed following the Pool Harbour plate design by Robert Jefferson in 1963. Some of the plates include; Hampshire, Jersey, Isle of Wight, Dorset, Beaulieu, Isle of Purbeck (designed by Ros Sommerfelt) and Bournemouth (Oakmead School) amongst others.

Many other locations, buildings and people were commissioned and appear on various shapes, including small rounded rectangular dishes and rounded triangular formed dishes.

Cathedral plates, designed by Tony Morris, in a Limited Editions of 1000, issued with certificates and presentation boxes.

Adoration of the Magi 1975. £200-£300/$330-$585.

Christ on the Cross 1975. £200-£300/$330-$585.

Flight into Egypt 1975. £150-£250/$245-$485.

Passion of Christ 1975. £200-£300/$330-$585.

Thomas A'Beckett charger. Limited Edition of 25, issued by Ricemans of Canterbury. £400-£700/$660-$1365.

Medieval Calender plates, designed by Tony Morris, in a Limited Edition of 1000, issued with certificates and boxed.

January 1972. £200-£400/$330-$780.

February 1972. £150-£200/$245-$390.

March 1972. £100-£200/$165-$390.

April 1973. £100-£200/$165-$390.

May 1974. £100-£200/$165-$390.

June 1974. £100-£200/$165-$390.

July 1975. £150-£200/$245-$390.

August 1975. £150-£220/$245-$430.

September 1975. £150-£220/$245-$430.

October 1975. £150-£200/$245-$390

November 1975. £150-£200/$245-$390.

December 1975. £100-£200/$165-$390.

Pattern Guide to Table Ware Ranges

Traditional tablewares – Possibly designed by John Adams, early 1920s, with floral designs by Truda Adams.

Purbeck tea ware – Designed by John Adams between 1930-33.

Studland tablewares – Designed by Harold Stabler, 1930.

Everest tea wares – Introduced in the early 1930s.

Picotee tableware – Introduced in the 1930s.

Wimborne ware – Designed by John Adams in the 1940s.

Ariel ware – Introduced in the 1930s.

Streamline tablewares – Designed by John Adams (1935-36). Updated by Alfred Read, with circular knop design and rimless plates (1953-55). Two-tone ranges renamed Twintone in the 1950s. Pebble design in black or grey, 1959.

Sherbourne Range – Designed by John Adams in the late 1930s and introduced into production in 1949.

Dorset range – Variation of Streamline supplied exclusively to Heal & Son, 1936-40.

Oven-to-Table ware- Designed by Robert Jefferson, 1960, launched 1961. Lucullus range, designed in 1961, launched 1962. Herb Garden, designed in 1961, launched 1963.

Contour tableware – Designed by Robert Jefferson, 1963-64. Desert Song range by Pat Summers 1960s. Morocco by Tony Morris, 1969.

Compact tableware – Designed by Robert Jefferson, 1965 and available until 1992 in Parkstone glaze and Broadstone glaze. Lids remodelled by Tony Morris in 1969.

Bokhara – Designed by Tony Morris in 1964. Consisted of jars and boxes with covers and vases.

Sea Crest tableware accessories – Designed by Tony Morris and Guy Sydenham, 1967-68.

Blue Lace tableware accessories – Designed by Tony Morris and Guy Sydenham, 1967-68.

New Stoneware coffee set – Designed by Guy Sydenham, 1967.

Oven Ware range – Available between 1975 and 1994.

The Style Range – Designed by Robert Jefferson, in production between 1979 and 1988.

The Flair Range – Designed by the Queensberry Hunt Partnership and available from 1983 until 1986.

The Concert Range – Designed by Elaine Williamson and the Poole design team, available between 1985 to 1992.

Astral – Designed by John Horler (Queensberry Hunt Partnership) available between 1989/1990.

Campden – Designed by Robert Welsh, 1989-91.

Next – Late 1980s.

Homespun ovenware – Designed by Alan White in 1989.

Microlyte ware – Designed by Trevor Wright, 1988-90.

Dorset Fruit – Designed by Alan Clarke in 1990.

Morning Glory shape – Designed in 1994 and still being used in 1999. After this shape/pattern new shape designs, Ranges or Collections as they are sometimes referred to in the promotional literature, seem to become nameless, there being a reliance on pattern name instead which can appear on either of the above or indeed new nameless shapes.

Pattern Designs – 1992 to Present

Arden – 1975-76.

Argosy – 1975-76.

Cyclamen – 1975-76.

Lagoon – 1975-76.

Sherwood – 1975-76.

Vortex – 1975-76.

Legumes – Designed by Sarah Chalmers (freelance), 1992.

Black Horse mug – Commission for Lloyds Bank plc, 1993.

Brush Stokes Floral – Designed by Anita Harris (freelance), 1992.

Gypsy – Designed by Anita Harris (freelance), 1992.

Reflections – Designed by Anita Harris (freelance), 1992.

Vineyard – Designed by Anita Harris (freelance), 1993.

Blue Vine – Designed by Anita Harris (freelance), 1993.

Blue Leaf – Designed by Anita Harris (freelance), 1994.

Green Leaf – Designed by Anita Harris (freelance), 1994.

Barley – Designed by Anita Harris (freelance), 1994, for Whittards, Chelsea.

Winter Vine – Designed by Anita Harris (freelance), 1994.

Vincent – Designed by Anita Harris (freelance), 1994.

Acorn and Oak Leaves – Designed by Anita Harris (freelance), 1994, for the National Trust.

Polka – Designed by Queensberry Hunt, 1994.

Morning Glory – Designed by Nicola Wiehahn, 1994.

Stourhead – Designed by Julie Depledge, for the National Trust, 1991.

Nasturtium – Desinged by Bryony Langworth, 1991.

Alfama – Designed by Anita Harris (freelance), for Tiffany & Co, 1994.

Tiffany Tulips – Designed by Anita Harris (freelance), for Tiffany & Co, 1992.

Tiffany Spice – Designed by Anita Harris (freelance), for Tiffany & Co, 1994.

Peony – Designed by Anita Harris (freelance), for Tiffany & Co, 1994.

New York Toile – Designed by Anita Harris (freelance), for Tiffany & Co, 1994.

Orchard – Designed by Kate Byrne, 1994.

Gold leaf – Introduced 1994.

New England – Designed by Anita Harris (freelance), 1995.

Charlotte – Designed by Anita Harris (freelance), 1995.

Sweet Pea – Designed by Anita Harris (freelance), 1996, made for the National Trust.

Calabash – Designed by Anita Harris (freelance), 1995.

Seed Packets – Introduced 1996 after designs of American seed packets from the late 1800s.

Omega – Designed by Fenella Mallalieu, 1997.

Country Rose – Designed by Lindsey Stevens, 1996, for MFI.

Highland Cattle – Designed by Anita Harris (freelance), 1996.

Sheep – Designed by Anita Harris (freelance), 1996 the above two being designed for Edinburgh Woollen Mills.

Terracotta – Designed by Rachel Barker and Andrew Brickett with Alan White, 1997.

Fresco – Designed by Rachel Barker and Andrew Brickett, (a colour variation using a chilli in place of the olive was made for Heal's) 1997.

Cranborne – Designed by Rachel Barker and Andrew Brickett, for Laura Ashley, 1997.

Rustic Wash – Adapted by Anita Harris after a design by Rachel Barker and Andrew Brickett, for Alders, 1998.

Sahara – Designed by Anita Harris, for Alders, 1998.

Bluebell – Designed by Anita Harris, for Marks & Spencer, 1998.

Woodland White – Designed by Anita Harris, for Marks & Spencer, 1998.

Fleur – Designed by Anita Harris, for Harrods, 1997.

Chickens – Designed by Anita Harris, for BHS (British Home Stores), 1998.

Fresco Wash – Designed by Rachel Barker and Andrew Brickett, 1997.

Citrus Grove – Designed by Anita Harris, for BHS 1998.

Faberge – Designed by Anita Harris, for MFI 1996.

Ferruccio – Designed by Anita Harris, for MFI 1996.

Vermont – Designed by Anita Harris, for MFI 1996.

Da Vinci – Designed by Anita Harris, for MFI 1995.

Matisse – Designed Sue Green (Queensberry Hunt Partnership), adapted by Anita Harris, for MFI 1995.

Bellini – Designed by Anita Harris, for MFI 1995.

Indigo – Designed by Anita Harris, for MFI 1995.

Fraiche – Designed by Anita Harris, adapted for the airbrush method by Alan Clarke, 1998.

Moonlight – Designed by Alan Clarke, for Alders, 1998.

Clouds – Designed by Alan Clarke, for John Lewis partnership, 1996.

Shadow Stripe – Designed by Alan Clarke, for John Lewis Partnership, 1997.

Glen Baxter – Mugs and plates, Introduced 1995.

Liberty Year mug – 1998, transfer print taken from Liberty & co archive.

Gardening – One of series of mugs for the Museum of Garden History, 1995.

Java – Designed by Anita Harris, 1998.

Late – Designed by Anita Harris, 1998.

Green Leaf – Designed by Anita Harris, 1998.

Pattern Guide to Gift and Ornamental Ware – 1970s to Present

Contrast Design developed by Leslie Elsden, 1977. 19 shapes in the range, mainly vases, bowls and dishes.

Sienna Designed and developed by Tony Morris and Jacqueline Leonard, 1978. 20 pieces in the range, mainly vases, bowls and plant pots.

Olympus Designed by Rosalind (Ros) Sommerfelt, 1977. 12 pieces in the range with Rosalinde and Seashore pattern.

Calypso Developed by Leslie Elsden, 1977-78. 18 pieces in the range.

Domino Introduced in 1976-77. 14 pieces – vases, bowls, plant pots and trays.

Beardsley Designed by Ros Sommerfelt, 1979. Initially 16 pieces, 11 more piece added in the following two years.

Fleurie Design by Ros Sommerfelt, transfers printed Mucha-style female heads, applied to Beardsley collection shapes. 1979-80.

The Country Lane Produced between 1979-83 on the Beardsley shapes.

Wild Garden Designed by Elaine Williamson, 1981, produced in the Beardsley shapes.

Bow Bells Designed by Ros Sommerfelt, 1981, produced in the Beardsley shapes.

Wren & Robin Designed by Barbara Linley Adams, 1982-84, produced in the Beardsley shapes.

Kandy Designed by Ros Sommerfelt,1982-83, produced in the Beardsley shapes.

Camelot plates Lady of Shalott and Arthur and Guinevere designed by Ros Sommerfelt. Voyage to Avalon and Excalibur designed by Tony Morris, 1977 (8½ins).

Calypso Queensberry Hunt Partnership, introduced 1984. A 'pastel' range was issued initially followed by 'plain' and 'lustre' monochrome coloured wares available from 1987. Later six decorated vases were issued, 1990.

Corinthian Queensberry Hunt Partnership, 1987. Monochrome fluted vases.

Cello vases Queensberry Hunt Partnership, 1990. Four shaped vases with differing marbleised finishes.

Fruit Cocktail Queensberry Hunt Partnership, 1990. Grecian and trumpet shaped vases with sponge fruit patterns.

Aztec vases Decorated with a Mary Jones Design pattern by Liane Huthchings, 1988-89.

Studio vases – **Athens** Designed by Ros Sommerfelt, stylised tulips, 1986. **Carnation** Designed by Sara Pearch, 1991. **Classic** Designed by Anita Harris, 1993.

Black and Gilt vase. Egyptian scene designed by Karen Hickisson on a hand thrown vase by Alan White, 1977 (19½ins).

Unnamed dish – Designed by Phillip Sutton, a full female face amongst stylised flowers, 1986 (16ins diameter).

Scenic Plates – There were in excess of 250 different scenes designed on sets of four, six and eight plates between 1983 and 1994. In all there were over 47 scenic plate sets produced during this period which would make it prohibitive to try and list them all.

Bone China giftware (interesting to see that Shell dish and Shell vase are still in production having been introduced in the early 1930s.).

Rosalind Designed by Elaine Williamson and Ros Sommerfelt, 1983-87.

Iona Designed by Elaine Williamson and Ros Sommerfelt, 1986-87.

Athena Designed by Elaine Williamson and Ros Sommerfelt, 1986-87.

The Ophelia Designed by Elaine Williamson, 1983-87.

Cymbeline Designed by Elaine Williamson, 1984-87.

Trelissick Designed by Elaine Williamson, 1986-87.

Pattern Guide to Poole Studio Collection – 1995 to Present

Gala Day dish – Designed by Sally Tuffin, exclusive to Poole Pottery club members, 1995.

Strolling Leopard – Year vase, designed by Sally Tuffin, exclusive to club members, 1995.

Parasols vase – Designed by Sally Tuffin, exclusive to club members, 1996.

Parasols dish – Designed by Sally Tuffin, exclusive to club members, 1996.

Gala Day dish – Designed by Sally Tuffin, exclusive to club members, 1996.

The Yaffle bowl – Designed by Sally Tuffin, available to club members, 1996.

Forrest Deer – Year vase, designed by Sally Tuffin, exclusive to club members, 1996.

Flags charger – Designed by Sally Tuffin, 1996.

Flags vase and cover – Designed by Sally Tuffin, 1996.

Seagull – Vase, designed by Sally Tuffin, 1996.

Seagull – Large dish, designed by Sally Tuffin, 1996.

Seagull – Medium dish, designed by Sally Tuffin, 1996.

Seagull – Small dish, designed by Sally Tuffin, 1996.

Fish – Vase, designed by Sally Tuffin, 1996.

Fish – Vase and cover, designed by Sally Tuffin, 1996.

Fish – Large dish, designed by Sally Tuffin, 1996.

Fish – Medium dish, designed by Sally Tuffin, 1996.

Fish – Small dish, designed by Sally Tuffin, 1996.

Bird – Vase, designed by Sally Tuffin, 1996.

Bird – Large dish, designed by Sally Tuffin, 1996.

Bird – Medium dish, designed by Sally Tuffin, 1996.

Bird – Small dish, designed by Sally Tuffin, 1996.

Brede Class Lifeboat plate – Year plate, designed by Sally Tuffin, club members, 1997.

Blue Poole – Vase and dish, designed by Sally Tuffin, for British Airways, (this design was used on a British Airways aircraft) 1997.

Arizona Blue – Designed by Sir Terry Frost, 1996.

Trewellard Red – Designed by Sir Terry Frost, 1996.

Isle of Purbeck series by Karen Brown:-

Old Harry Rocks vase – exclusive to club members (16cms), 1997.

Old Harry Rocks vase – exclusive to club members (8ins), 1998.

Old Harry Rocks vase – (25cm), 1998.

Old Harry Rocks dish – exclusive to club members, 1998.

Old Harry Rocks dish – (25cms), 1998.

Old Harry Rocks dish – (42cm), 1998.

Corfe Castle vase – exclusive to club members (8ins), 1998.

Corfe Castle dish – exclusive to club members, 1998.

Viking Ships vase – exclusive to club members (8ins), 1998.

Viking Ships vase – (25cm), 1998.

Viking Ships dish – exclusive to club members, 1998.

Viking Ships dish – (25cm), 1998.

Viking Ships dish – (42cm), limited edition, 1998.

Lotus vase – Athens shape, special offer to members, (8ins), 1998.

Lotus vase – (36cm), 1998.

Lotus vase – (25cm), 1998.

Lotus dish – (17cm), 1998.

Lotus dish – (26cm), 1998.

Lotus dish – (32cm), 1998.

Gala Day Caro vase – Athens shape, special offer to members (8ins), 1998.

Gala Day Caro dish – special offer to members, 1998.

Charlotte Mellis

Blue Wash – Charlotte Mellis, from 1997.

Green Wash – Charlotte Mellis, from 1997.

Blue/Yellow Wash – Charlotte Mellis, from 1997.

Dolphin Tankard – Designed by Alan White for the Poole Collectors Club, 1997.

Carp Dish – Designed by Alan Clarke, limited edition of 250 available exclusively to club members, 1997.

Janice Tchalenko: Introduced three ranges in 1996.

Yellow Flower – A vase (21cm), three dishes (32cm, 26cm and 17cm) and a ginger jar (23cm).

Blue Flower – A vase (21cm), three dishes (32cm, 26cm, and 17cm) and a ginger jar (23cm).

Red Flower – A vase (21cm), three dishes (32cm, 26cm and 17cm) and a ginger jar (23cm).

New Delphis – Designed by Anita Harris and Alan Clarke, together with Janice Tchalenko using the 'Living Glaze' technique. 1999. A tall flared vase, a ginger jar and cover and a wall plaque.

Eclipse – Designed by Alan Clarke using the 'Living Glaze' technique. Three dishes, 25cm, 35cm and 42cm, each produced in a limited edition of 1999 pieces of each shape, boxed with certificates. 1999.

Millennium – Designed by Alan Clarke using the 'Living Glaze' technique. Two dishes, 25cm and 42cm and an Egyptian vase, 35cm high, each being produced in a limited edition of 2000 pieces boxed with certificates. 1999.

Nursery Wares

1921 appears to be the year in which nursery ware designs were first created at Poole with designs by Harold Stabler, John and Truda Adams and Dora Batty. As with other potteries demand fluctuated over the decades with new designs being created following a response from the public or the introduction of new designers interested in promoting or up-dating the company's range. The wares themselves range from tea wares such as bowls, mugs, plates and egg-cups through to the large toilet sets. Many of the designs, as previously mentioned, were also used to decorate tiles and were hand-painted and coloured until the 1960s.

Waterbirds series – Harold Stabler, circa 1921.

Nursery Toys series – Dora Batty, circa 1921-22.

Animals series – Truda Adams, 1920s.

Nursery Rhymes – Dora Batty, circa 1934.

The Zoo – Eileen McGrath, 1934-35.

The Picnic – Eileen McGrath, 1934-35.

The Circus – Eileen McGrath, 1934-35. (This should not be confused with the tile designs by Clifford and Rosemary Ellis.)

London Characters – Truda Carter, 1934-35.

Kensington Gardens – Truda Carter, 1934-35.

Toys – Truda Carter, circa 1934.

Play Box – Alfred Read, circa 1935.

Animal set – Robert Jefferson, screen-printed black and white designs on yellow and blue grounds, 1962.

Nursery Rhymes – Elaine Williamson, transfer printed set, 1979.

My Little Pony set – Elaine Williamson for Hambro Industries , 1985.

The Mad Hatters Tea Party – Sarah Chalmers, boxed sets, 1994.

Tile Price Guide
1917 to the Present

The following list of tiles by various designers is only meant to be a representative selection rather than a complete list.

Blue Dutch (£35-£60/$55-$115 each) and **Coloured Dutch** (£35-£60/$55-$115 each) series designed by Joseph Roelants, possibly from as early as 1917. There are twelve designs known in this series produced in blue or coloured versions executed by hand painting. Later produced using silk-screen printing in the late 1950s and 1960s (later blue version, £25-£45/$40-$85 Coloured £25-£45/$40-$85).

Blue Boats series (£35-£60/$55-$115). This appears to be a far rarer hand painted design by Roelant's, probably dating from the same period and was also produced in as a **Coloured Boat** series (£35-£60/$55-$115). As with the previous Dutch series, these were also later to be produced by the silk-screen method (later blue version, £25-£45/$40-$85. Coloured £25-£45/$40-$85).

Nursery Rhymes (£25-£45/$40-$85) and **Nursery Toys** (£25-£45/$40-$85) tile series designed by Dora Batty during the early 1920s. Another nursery series, **Playbox** (£35-£60/$55-$115) was designed by A. B. Read although probably slightly later on in the 1930s. These were also later to be produced using screen prints from the 1950s onwards.

The Chase (£30-£60/$50-$115) and **Sporting** (£30-£60/$50-$115) designed by Edward Bawden in the early 1920s. Both of these series were hand painted and could still be ordered in to the 1950s, although the later editions were very different.

Waterbirds series designed by Harold Stabler between 1921-25. Hand painted, these designs can also be found on Nursery tablewares, and were still being produced on tiles in the 1950s.

Farmyard series designed by E. E. Strickland in about 1922. One of the most commonly seen and well known of these early pictorial tiles. There were single tile or four tile versions, the latter being ordered for all the Dewhurst and Mac Fisheries retailers around Britain. For the single tiles £35-£55/$55-$105 (later versions £20-£30/$35-$60) and for the four tile panels £70-£100/$115-$195 (later versions £40-£70/$65-$135).

Seagull possibly by Irene Fawkes.

POTTERY—BRITISH

A selection of Carter & Co Ltd tile designs - Nursery Rhymes by Dora Batty, Water Birds by Harold Stabler, Flowers by Truda Adams. Studio Yearbook, 1924.

Caller Herrin' by Dora M Batty. (£35-£50/$55-$95)

Fishing Smacks by Minnie McLeish. (£35-£50/$55-$95)

Three tile designs developed as a consequence of the Farmyard series, all designed between 1921 and 1925 and made for use by Mac Fisheries. These designs along with four others were used on pot lids. All three were stencilled.

The Ship designed by Harold Stabler, circa 1925, using a faience tile covered with silver lustre, (8ins square), (£60-£90/$100-$175).

Dairy tile panels designed by Arthur Nickols, 1920s, (£50-£80/$80-$155).

Fish designed by Arthur Nickols, 1930s, (£30-£50/$50-$95).

Alphabet series, possibly designed by Reginald Till, 1920s. Tube-lined (£50-£80/$80-$155).

Pelican designed by Truda Carter, 1920s, (£40-£70/$65-$135).

Flowers designed by Truda Carter and Reginald Till, 1920s, (£600-£900/$990-$1755). Truda Carter adapting her colourful designs from her tablewares for tiles. During this period there were various floral tile series, two being produced by Reginald Till and others by Truda Carter, with other versions designs into the 1950s.

Grapes & Vine designed by Erna Manners or Truda Adams, early 1920s. (£50-£80/$80-$155)

W. H. Smith promotional tile panels, dating from the 1920s. Designer unknown. (£100-£200/$165-$390).

Florida designed by Reginald Till in the 1920s. Sunburst effect motif from a combination of green, blue and/or Salmon being thrown onto a thick buff tile. (£50-£80/$80-$155)

London Underground tiles designed by Harold Stabler between 1938-39. In all there were eighteen designs each moulded in low relief depicting well known buildings; St Paul's, House of Parliament, etc as well as motifs such as the circle and line design of the London Underground. (£60-£120/$100-$235)

Dogs tile designs by **Cecil Aldin**, (£35-£50/$55-$95 each. Six in all). Freelance artists were used frequently at Carter & Co as has already been seen, and these, dating from the 1930s, are typical examples. Unusually the designs appear with the artist's facsimile signature.

Poole Swimming Club stoneware plaque by Reginald Till or A Nikols, dating from 1932. (£80-£180/$130-$350)

Dolphin leaping over bottle kiln designed by A Nikols, 1930s. (£80-£120/$130-$235).

Fishes tube-lined panel, 1930s, designer unknown. (£150-£250/$245-$485)

Golfing tile panel, 1930s, stencilled designer unknown. (£150-£250/$245-$485)

Children's Clock face unknown designer, c.1935 (£100-£200/$165-$390). In 1995 a rare tube-lined four tile panel clock face was discovered. The numbers appeared against variously coloured circular balloon-like images, with the body of a clown standing in the middle, wearing a red peaked hat and a star studded yellow ground costume. The clown had no arms, as these would have been made out of metal to form the hands of the clock. As the clock was not pierced in the center for the spindle to protrude through to rotate the arms, I think it is safe to assume that this particular set of tiles never fulfilled their ultimate task.

Hospital Tiling

The Lord Mayor Treloar Hospital, Alton, Hants.
Eight tiled fire places, installed in the 1930s. These consisted of a central picture of four tiles with individual tiles. The designs were executed by E.E. Strickland and Joseph Roelants and are taken from the Farmyard series by Strickland and the Dutch figures in rural scenes by Roelants.

Hemel Hempstead Hospital, West Herts.
Installed in the children's ward in about 1939, there are ten panels depicting animals wearing various human clothes, hats, bow ties, etc. Eight panels are 1' 6' by 1' and two are 3' 6" by 1'. They depict a fox, a piglet, a tortoise and hare, a giraffe, a camel, an elephant, a rhino, an owl, a duck and a cock and hen.

Heswell Hospital, Merseyside.
There are various manufacturers involved in the three areas of tiling here, Carters seem likely to have carried out some of the animal and children designs in one of the rooms. The hospital closed in 1985 and the tiling has hopefully been re-installed in the Liverpool Alder Hey hospital for Children by this time.

Bolingbroke Hospital, Wandsworth, London.
The main tiling here is the thirteen Simpson Nursery Rhyme panels. There are four smaller panels by Carters, dating from 1925-6, of animals in human clothing. Alligator in black trousers and a blue coat, Lion in blue trousers and a green coat, Monkey riding an ostrich and an Alligator in red trousers and a grey jacket.

King Edward Memorial Hospital, Ealing, London.
There are some fifteen panels, dating from 1934, painted by Phyllis Butler, senior paintress at the time, depicting various nursery rhymes, a biblical panel and two panels of the Royal Princesses, Elizabeth and Margaret thatched cottage. The largest panel being 8' by 5' and the smallest 4' 6" by 4'.

Guys Hospital, London
There are some twenty-six panels still in situ in part of the hospital no longer used for children, all the panels depict nursery rhymes themes and date from the early 1930s.

The Middlesex Hospital, London.
Described as probably Carters biggest single contract, the commission called for the new West Wing of the Middlesex Hospital, dating from 1930, to have almost all of its wall, floors and corridors tiled by Carters. There are nineteen pictorial panels of village scenes, animals, pets and nursery rhymes, with the largest panel All the Fun of the Fair, designed by a Mr Hadyn Jensen, almost covering a whole wall, measuring 26' by 7' 6". This huge panel also used a technique never used at Carters before described In the Carters 1935

CARTER *Hand Printed Tiling*

at Hainault Forest Secondary School, Essex.

Architects: F. R. S. Yorke, F.R.I.B.A., E. Rosenberg, F.R.I.B.A. and C. S. Mardall, A.R.I.B.A.

Contractors: F. R. Hipperon & Son Ltd.

The tile shown on the left is used in conjunction with plain tiles of the darker colour for the general wall treatment, and another hand printed tile is used to form the frieze. The tiles were designed and arranged by Peggy Angus.

CARTER

Peggy Angus hand printed tile design and scheme for the Hainault Forest Secondary School, Essex. Design magazine, 1953.

Peggy Angus tile designs for Carter & Co Ltd, making use of a simple diagonal pattern design in different colours which can be used to produce numerous geometric panels. Design magazine, 1953.

hospital tile brochure as "Flat masses of bright colours were desired, masses applied in what we think of as the poster manner....."

Poole District General Hospital, Poole, Dorset

In 1970, in their own back garden, although under the name of Pilkington, Carters were able to contribute to the main entrance corridor with a series of pictures of stylised flowers in shades of brown against off white tiles when the new hospital was built.

Kent and Sussex Hospital, Tunbridge Wells, Kent.

Completed in about 1934 when the building was opened, there would appear to have been almost thirty panels in this scheme which consisted of a main panel of a big Noah's Ark, 5' 6" by 3' 6", with numerous smaller panels of various animals and nursery rhymes.

Maesteg General Hospital, Maesteg, West Glamorgan.

The children's ward was built in 1926 and the tiling completed in 1936. The tile scheme consisted of a variety of animals in human clothing, painted in a two tile high frieze bordered by dark blue tiles, heading for a large Ark at the end of the ward. One other large panel depicts The Old Woman who lived in a Shoe.

St Helier Maternity Hospital, St Helier, Jersey.

Here are two panels unlike previous Carters designs. Dated 1925 and initialled J.R.Y. for James Radley Young, the two panels depict Christ blessing children and a girl gazing at a fairy wedding with hares and elves.

Tile Price Lists

The following list of tiles by various designers is only meant to be a representative selection rather than a complete list.

1950s – Picture Tiles

Sea Plants By Phyllis Butler £10-£15/$15-$30 each

Sea By Susan Williams-Ellis. £10-£15/$15-$30 each

Nursery Toys By Dora Batty. £15-£30/$25-$60 each

Sporting By Edward Bawden. £15-£30/$25-$60 each

Clifford and Rosemary Ellis Circus tile designs, hand-painted, for Carter & Co Ltd. Design magazine, 1953.

Dutch Scenes By Joseph Roelants. £40-£80/$65-$155 each

Play Box By Alfred Read. £20-£40/$35-$80 each

Fish By A. Nickols. £20-£40/$35-$80 each

English Countryside By Reginald Till £20-£35/$35-$70 each

Farmyard By E. E. Strickland. £10-£20/$15-$40 each

Flowers By Truda Carter and Reginald Till. £10-£20/$15-$40 each

Kitchen By Alfred Read. £10-£20/$15-$40 each

Pub Games By Reginald Till. £15-£30/$25-$60 each

Chase By Edward Bawden. £30-£60/$50-$115 each

Water Birds By Harold Stabler. £20-£40/$35-$80 each

Dogs By Cecil Aldin. £20-£40/$35-$80 each

Ships By Reginald Till. £10-£15/$15-$30 each

Nursery Rhymes By Dora Batty. £15-£30/$25-$60 each

The Circus designed by Clifford and Rosemary Ellis, early 1950s. This series included a sealion, a kangaroo, a zebra, a horse two trapeze artists and two clowns, with a four-tile central panel of a female figure standing on the back of a horse with a ring master, all within circus ring. Single tile – £15-£30/$25-$60. Panel – £40-£80/$65-$155.

1950s

Peggy Angus – 'Classic Range'. Silk screen printed and designed between 1950-55. Still in use in the late 1960's. Black and white repeat designs of circular abstract motifs. Also included are designs using simple a wavy line, large dots, diagonally divided pattern produced in various colour-ways (CPR608 to CPR611). £30-£50/$50-$95.

Commemorative. 1953. Screen printed, Coronation of Queen Elizabeth II. (£20-£30/$35-$60)

Cupid & Dolphin 1950s. Screen printed, designer unknown. (£20-£30/$35-$60)

1958-64

Silk screen prints by various artists internal and freelance, including:

Ivor Kamlish – sgraffito cross-hatch design (PR484), horizontal broken bands (PR521), irregular lines of dots (PR490), repeated atomic motif (PR517), segmented lines in bands with line through the middle of each band (PR486), two segmented compressed circle (PR414) and square divided into sixteen squares each with six rectangular sections (PR522). All produced in various colours, 1955-65. £30-£60/$50-$115.

Robert Nicholson – Freelance. Vertical lines crossed with single and double lines, better known as 'barbwire' design (PR378). Produced in various colours, c1955. £30-£60/$50-$115.

A. B. Read – Repeated small black outlined diamond motifs inside similar shapes in light and shade (PR302). £30-£60/$50-$115.

Gordon Cullen – Freelance. Light and shade twisted vertical bands on shaded ground (PR127) and a stylised floral diagonal repeat pattern (PR268), 1958-60. £30-£60/$50-$115.

Laurence Scarfe – Freelance. Produced four geometric repeat patterns of kaleidoscopic form, as part of the Classic Range (CPR616 to CPR619), 1960. £30-£60/$50-$115.

Textured Tiles

Designs for these were initially created by **Ivor Kamlish** (TS1 & TS2) and later added to by **A.B. Read**. These were produced by moulding the surface pattern in the form of repeated rectangular depressions with diagonal sections (TS1) creating light and shade areas within each rectangular and repeated lines of ovals (TS2) again creating light and dark areas, each changing with the direction of the light source. Both having a value of £20-£50/$35-$95.

1960s – Picture Tiles

Fauna by Sylvia Ball. £10-£15/$15-$30 each

Lakeland by Phyllis Butler. £10-£15/$15-$30 each

Pub Games by Reginald Till. £15-£20/$25-$40 each

Fish by A. Nickols. £15-£20/$25-$40 each

Cookery by Claire Wallis. £10-£15/$15-$30 each

Field Grasses by Phyllis Butler. £15-£25/$25-$50 each

English Countryside by Reginald Till. £10-£15/$15-$30 each

Sea Plants by Phyllis Butler. £10-£15/$15-$30 each

Pet Dogs by Margaret Matthews. £10-£15/$15-$30 each

Flora by Phyllis Butler. £10-£15/$15-$30 each

Veteran Cars by Margaret Matthews. £10-£15/$15-$30 each

Herbs by Margaret Matthews. £10-£15/$15-$30 each

Sea by Susan Williams-Ellis. £10-£15/$15-$30 each

Farmyard by E. E. Strickland. £35-£55/$55-$105 each

Birds by Peggy Angus.£350-£450/$575-$875 each

1964 – Picture Tiles

Several of the above 'Picture Tile' series were still being advertised; **Fauna**, **Veteran Cars**, **Herbs** and **Field Grasses**. New designs included a set of **Zodiac** tiles (£6-£10/$10-$20), **Alphabet** tiles (£10-£15/$15-$30) as well as new designs for the **Kitchen** (£10-£15/$15-$30), **Carriages** (£10-£15/$15-$30), **Ships** (£10-£15/$15-$30), **English Countryside** (£10-£15/$15-$30), **Fishes** (£15-£20/$25-$40) and others all making use of the silk screen process. New designers including Una Hart, Brian Moore and Daphne Padden, amongst others, created some of these designs.

The tiles mentioned above were all very much part of everyday production, being produced in large numbers for both retail outlets as well as for architectural commissions. Special commissions also played a large part of the output of the Hamworthy decorative wares departments. Individual productions varied from those designed and modelled by Tony Morris in the Faience department, where he produced various sized slabs modelled in low-relief with fish, plankton shells, and other crustacean (1967) to individual rectangular faience tiles with unique abstract hand painted patterns, which can still be seen on the outside walls of the pottery (1963). Other tile designs by Tony Morris include a recently discovered framed twenty-eight tile panel decorated with a wonderful abstract design using Delphis colouring and possibly dates from the late 1960s.

1970s

Mask series by Leslie Elsden (£15-£30/$25-$60). Printed in black on a white ground. The same designer also created a series of scenes or views of streets, rivers, etc making use of a red stoneware body (£10-£15/$15-$30). These dated to between 1977 to 1979.

Delphis tiles – painted by Janet Laird, c1972. £15-£30/$25-$60.

Marks

As with any other long standing major ceramic manufacturer the number of marks used throughout it's long history are extremely varied and often inaccurate in terms of dating. Marks supposedly stopped in a certain year, especially printed ones, continued to be used along side new marks for many months and sometimes years. At Poole they used the whole gambit of methods of marking from impressed stamps, hand incised marks, printed, painted, stencilled and screen printed. Some marks were specifically used on only one type or range of wares and even for only one year whilst other marks were in use for 30 or 40 years. Just to add to the complexity there are several other marks relating to the shape, thrower, paintresses, designers, trial marks and more. In recent years the identification and listing of the painters and paintresses has become increasingly important to many collectors. No longer just satisfied with collecting a certain type, range or style of ware, many collectors are now seeking out certain painters and/or paintresses work in much the same manner as some of the Moorcroft pottery collectors.

For some collectors and dealers the two most useful marks are the shape number and the pattern code. It is only through a combination of letters and/or numbers that patterns and their various colour ways can be identified as specific pattern names were not generally used at Poole. Thus '343/FSU' equates to a angular waisted double cone vase decorated with 'stars' motifs of a certain colour. Inevitably, more recognisable and understandable names have become associated with many of the patterns, especially those associated with the 1950s Contemporary designs of Alfred Read, Ann Read and Ruth Pavely namely Butterflies, Bamboo, Loops, Tadpoles, Basket weave, etc.

For many years one of the tricks of the trade as an aid to identifying the approximate date of some of the Traditional ware has been the use of a pink coloured glaze inside and on the base of pieces. The use of this tinted glaze has been generally accepted to indicate a mid to late 1930s date. After this time Traditional ware had a white interior glaze and then from the late 1960s through the introduction of modern machinery and the refinement of raw materials

1951 saw the introduction of a new mark that was again associated with a change in management and staff at Poole, namely Lucien Myers and Alfred Read, as well as change in artistic direction. The initial mark can be seen in the centre of this impressed mark, namely POOLE over a Dolphin with ENGLAND beneath used from 1951 to 1955. The use of a Dolphin as part of a mark was first used on early lustre wares between 1900 and 1908. This mark, however, was not only used on the base of the wares but was also incorporated into all the advertising and promotional brochures, letter heads and anywhere else it could be used as part of a new corporate image. The mark illustrated here is the second version with Hand Made, Hand Decorated outside a circle and was used from 1952 to 1955. The use of these words outside the mark is indicative of the new higher profile status that the management at Poole wanted to project, at the same time reflecting public interest and demand for things 'Hand Made'.

Carter & Co - Initially incised from 1900 and then used as an impressed mark from about 1908 with the addition of 'Poole' in the mark. This impressed mark was used until 1921, the end of the first significant period at the Carter/Poole pottery after which the new partnership of Cater, Stabler and Adams evolved.

Carter, Stabler, Adams. Poole. England. This mark formed the bases for a new set of impressed marks used between 1921 and 1934, with one variation; POOLE over ENGLAND within a rectangle becoming a standard mark, although with later improvements, still in use today.

these wares generally began to become thinner and the glaze more matte and consistent.

Amongst all the marks there are a few essential marks that indicate important or significant alterations to the marks used at Poole which used with later variations for significant periods of time.

This hand painted mark, used between 1956 and 1959, came about as a consequence of the use of a black panther glaze.

From 1955 the 1951 mark was modernised with a slicker looking Dolphin and alteration to the graphics of the lettering. This mark and it's variations were in use until 1969. This mark or rather variations of it, was still in use in the late 1960s until 1972 were it can be found on the new ranges of Oven to Tablewares amongst other wares.

Another change in staff with the arrival of Robert Jefferson as designer saw another transformation in the mark. The changes, released in 1962, involved a further updating of the Dolphin mark with a new more realistic drawing and the incorporation of the word Studio into the mark. The use of the word Studio emphasises still further the type of work initiated through the work of Alfred Read, Guy Sydenham, Ann Read and Ruth Pavely. This particular mark with a line and england under the word Studio was used between 1964 and 1966. The initial mark of the re-drawn dolphin between POOLE and STUDIO was use from 1962 to 1964. Traditional wares and other wares that formed the main line of production used the same mark but with the word England replacing Studio. This mark being used between 1966 and 1980.

This impressed mark, POOLE ENGLAND, seen here on a piece of Atlantis ware, was initially used in 1974 and is still being used today. It is very much a continuation of a mark used on Poole since the mid 1920s.

As if to emphasis the winding down of the Studio and Hand Craft operations at Poole with the departure of various members of the Studio, a completely new approach to marking Poole was instigated in the late 1970s. Transfer printing now took over from traditional impressed and/or stamped marks. This change inaugurated a whole plethora of marks and variations that were possible through this method. Individually specific and/or limited runs of marks could be made with greater complexity. What is interesting to note is the return of the previous 1959 sleek dolphin motif as if to emphasis the longevity and trustworthiness of the old firm. This mark is one of the many transfer printed marks is use in more recent years. Also noteworthy is the return to more traditional use of caligraphy.

1995 saw the re-introduction of Studio ware at Poole through the new Poole Studio after a twenty-five year gap. This followed three years after the Management buy-out. Sally Tuffin fresh from transforming the fortunes of the Moorcroft Pottery between 1986 and 1992 was the first to create the new look at Poole. This mark dating from 1996, says much for the renewed emphasis and dynamism at Poole. Sir Terry Frost, RA, was asked to develop two designs for a limited production of 100 to be sold at the Royal Academy of Arts. The use of limited production pieces reflects the demand of the burgeoning collectors market of the 1980s and the fact that such a major fine artist was asked and agreed to carry out the commission extends a long tradition at Poole pottery. Another major contemporary artist working with Poole at this time is Janice Tchalenko.

Recent Trends and Developments

The Collecting of Poole Pottery has for many years been bubbling under the surface waiting to erupt. That it has remained in this state is due in part to a general lack of knowledge with only one serious book, relatively lacking in illustrations, being available from 1980 to 1995 together with the odd exhibition pamphlet. Collectors have developed into those that have built up large collections of inexpensive pieces in specific styles or those with a little foresight and self-developed knowledge who have built up more serious and expensive collections. The latter can almost be counted on one hand. The former group consists of a few hundred people or more and is also more International, unlike the serious collectors. At least that was the case until about 1993/5 when specific exhibitions and printed material started to develop. This higher profile was helped by a general growth in collecting post-war decorative arts, seen in the catalogues of Christie's South Kensington (10th September, 1990, Christie's first auction devoted entirely to Poole Pottery), as well as numerous exhibitions and books on or related to the 1950s and later 1960, specifically the 'New Look Design in the Fifties' by Lesley Jackson in 1991/92.

The Market

As far as the dealers, auction houses and collectors are concerned, the last few years have seen a marked increase in the interest and prices of certain types of Poole Pottery. The 1990 Christie's auction, mentioned above, had mixed results with just one lot reaching over £1,000, eleven lots exceeding £400 and the remainder averaging about £120. This sale, however, did much to kick-start a broader interest and awareness in Poole Pottery and its variety of wares. Naturally of course what had once been the relatively private collecting field of a few, grew into a highly competitive field, wares often over-priced with the lack of any clear price guidelines. This largely unrepresentative pricing of wares is part of what is seen as a predictable pattern or pricing waves of a new collectable field and something that has previously happened, in terms of ceramics, to Susie Cooper, Clarice Cliff, Moorcroft and such like. Only after a several months, sometimes years of irregular and irrational pricing are price bands slowly developed and adhered to, which then allows for a more interesting, steadily developing collector's market, largely born of confidence in 'reasonable market prices'. Personal collections can now be developed and this is the beauty of a pottery such as Poole. There are endless permutations of objects, styles, periods, colours, patterns and types of ware to collect thanks to the longevity of the firm.

Today things have settled down somewhat, at least into some sort of hierarchy of collectability. The most expensive wares, in order of prices, are the magnificent large French-inspired, Art Deco influenced vases and wall plaques dating from the late 1920s through to the mid 1930s, and the highly individual one-off designs of the Delphis Studio between 1963 and 1966, specifically large dishes by Robert Jefferson and Tony Morris. These are then followed by the rare early lustre wares, rare Atlantis pieces and many other usual and/or impressive pieces.

Something that Poole Pottery collectors, indeed many collectors, will pay a little extra for is a piece that has a traceable history, perhaps being made for a certain person, or that was exhibited at or even made for a major exhibition of the period, or is known to have once belonged to the designer, factory owner, etc. Premiums are often paid for this sort of item, therefore it would do the seller no harm to spend a little time and effort, if they think that the piece is important or substantial enough, in doing some research.

One-offs and trials

Most potteries have produced numerous one-off designs and trials which were often the inspiration for a new range or series of wares. These trials have frequently found their way onto the open market in various ways over the years. In former years (before 1940), it would have been normal practice to have either kept such unique pieces within the factory, or certainly within the family (if the firm was family owned) or alternatively to have smashed the wares, along with those that did not the exacting high production standards required. Even so, it is still quite amazing, or perhaps not so, to see vast numbers of 'unique' or 'trial' wares which constantly turn up on the market. Having interviewed numerous pottery workers over the years and having several such wares myself from five different potteries such 'escapes' become less remarkable. There are numerous reasons and accounts of how such 'gifts' left the factory, mostly quite legitimate and a few not. Practices varied from pot bank to pot bank, often according to the size or personal inclination of the managing director. Workers might be given wares on their retirement, after a certain number of years' service or on the occasion of some news or other. Fellow workers were sometimes allowed to club together and purchase certain wares for a fellow worker's leaving present. The run up to Christmas had certain traditions within certain potteries, with workers sometimes even being allowed to fire ware, limited to one or two pieces, that they had made themselves and/or decorated, as a present for a family member. This was certainly the case at Malkin tiles and Richards tiles. Trials that might have been painted by a certain worker and which were then not put into production might have available for purchase, having to be marked as a second with a steel, rather than be smashed.

Some of the less legitimate but none the less inventive, ways for wares to leave the factory included the wearing of braces and a jacket. Flat ware, such as plates, saucers and such, could be fastened to the braces, two one each side front and back, which when covered with a jacket could not be noticed. The worker could then freely stride out of the factory gates, his arms quite normally thrusting through the air. Anyway, I digress, as this sort of thing could never happen today.

Since the 1980s these highly commercial unique wares have been either deliberately held back for inclusion in special annual collectors club member only sales or auctions or even deliberately created for such events. Not that such trials, etc, have been deliberately created at the Poole Pottery but certainly elsewhere the high premiums paid for such items, along with the voracious collecting fad for limited editions, at other potteries has not gone unnoticed by some pottery managers.

At Poole Pottery there are also unique exhibition, trial and one-off non-production wares to be found. These wares do not include the individual Studio craft wares produced at Poole during the 1960s and 1970s which form an entirely different category.

A hand thrown vase with the Aubrey Beardsley pattern, painted by Susan Pottinger in 1978, is an example of a unique trial piece that eventually led to the development of the Bearsdley collection, introduced in 1979, all the pieces being manufactured by the slip-cast method.

Fakes and Restoration

At the time of writing there appears to be only one out and out fake (and there is no other word for it) namely a sculptural wall bracket. Some 12 to 13 inches high, this bracket is incised 'POOLE ENGLAND' and has been found in antique centres and provincial salerooms throughout Britain. The one I saw was in a Warwick Antique centre where I was able to get a closer look. The Collectors Club has illustrated the offending item in the Spring 1997 magazine. From what I saw, I can say that the glaze was altogether far too 'brilliant' or glossy, there was artificial staining in the glaze-crazing and the modelling lacked any detail. If you come across any of these pieces in the future you should contact Poole Pottery, making a note of the location, etc.

Restoration, as with any item made of ceramic, is always going to be an issue but until recently this was not one that Poole wares suffered from very often as the costs involved were usually more than the value of the item after restoration. More often than not even large, early or expensive wares were sold the with the damage untouched. Since the mid 1990s, however, with rising prices and more competition for rare and bigger pieces, the amount of restoration has increased. Poole pottery, especially the pre-1930s wares, were particularly susceptible to knocks as the earthenware body was not very high fired and used a comparatively thin glaze. As the company progressed and technical changes developed in an effort to reduce kiln losses and generally to improve reliability the body material and the glaze were altered and improved, especially as hand-thrown wares gave way to slip-cast mass-produced wares.

All commercial restoration can be spotted, no matter how good it is, if you teach yourself to look for it and how to identify it. All the restoration you are ever likely to come across is what is called 'plastic', meaning that it is made of a non-ceramic material and has not been fired. This makes the restoration easy to spot because it will always have a different surface to that of a fired ceramic surface. Ceramic wares are very hard and cold (unless they are sitting on a radiator), whereas restoration is soft and will be warm when touched for any length of time.

So how do you spot restoration? The first thing to do is to look at the piece, without picking it up, and ask yourself where the piece would be most likely to be knocked. The rim, the base, the widest part (usually the shoulder on a vase), the spout, the knop, the base of the handle, the neck of a figure, any extended parts of the body, these are all likely places. You will then be able to pick up the piece and examine it more closely, using an eye glass if you wish, although after a short time of spotting damage you will become more confident about recognising it and put the eye glass away. The most valuable tools you can ever use to spot restoration, cracks and chips are your fingers, eyes and teeth. Use your fingernails to lightly drag across an area you suspect might be restored, along the rim or base, and notice any changes in the freedom of movement or lack of it, across the surface of the ware. Restored areas will always have a different surface sheen or texture to that of the ceramic. In the case of Poole there are some wares, usually the earlier pre-1930, that have a slight matte, hard, thin glaze, which was and is more susceptible to damage, as mentioned above. Later alterations to the glaze helped to prevent such defects. You might should also be able to see restored areas, easier with practice of course, by the variation in colour tones or consistency of colour, as it is very, very difficult to exactly match in-glaze or even on-glaze colours that were in use thirty or forty years ago, especially as they are probably not available today. Once you think you might have located a repaired area, you can then check for warmth and sound. As restoration is made-up of plastic materials the restored area will hold and conduct heat therefore holding your hand over a suspect area, taking it away for a moment and then returning it highlight which parts of the body went cold and those that stayed warm. As a final indicator, you can gently tap your teeth against the surface of the suspect area to hear if it makes a sharp and hard ting, for a ceramic body, or a dull thud for a restored area. It may not sound like something to recommend but if you go to a major ceramic auction in London, New York or Wareham, you will probably see a few people seemingly biting into pieces of ceramics. It is very effective and it works.

All the above can only be gained through practice, so the more pieces you pick up and check the better. Even if you don't intend to buy a piece, the faster and more efficiently you can master the art of detecting restoration the quicker you will save money. Even if you find, by looking at pieces you already have, that you have unknowingly purchased restored items and there is little you can do about it (although do try to return such items if recently bought as the seller may not have been aware and could themselves do something about it), you can at least learn from the experience.

There is nothing whatsoever wrong with buying restored, chipped, cracked items so long as you are aware of the fact and the item is, in your view, correctly priced to reflect that fact. There are plenty of collectors who might well pay hundreds, even thousands of pounds for a damaged item, if they know the rarity of the piece and assess that the price is acceptable. There are numerous reasons for collecting, such as purely for decorative effect, where damage is less of consideration than price, but I won't go into these. The reasons for what and how you collect are entirely personal, I just hope that the above might come in useful.

Poole and the Internet

As has been seen in the previous chapters Poole has now become one of the latest 'collectable' areas, having a diversity of material, sufficient pieces available on the market and broad enough piece range to appeal to a wide range of collectors.

This diversity and breadth is something that is very well reflected on the Internet, specifically the various on-line auction web sites. Poole has yet to develop the useful, informative collectors fan-type pages, with one or two exceptions, and is largely found through a search as a reference to an auction site. The obvious site to find historical and current information on Poole Pottery is their on web site as I have previously mentioned.

It has not taken long for Poole pieces to find ready buyers on the largest Internet auction sites such as ebay, where large rare wall plaques, 16 inches, dating from the early Delphis period are already fetching £800/$1575, whereas a similar dated and decorated Delphis dish but only an 8 inches sells for £50/$80. I have already mentioned that a trial Atlantis vase recently sold in America for £1035/$1975 (excluding shipping and insurance) to a UK buyer.

What can be seen from the Internet auction sites is that there are plenty of pieces in Australia, Canada, North America and of course Britain. The biggest buyers and sellers are British but with the restrictive costs of shipping, certainly in relation to lower value items, this can be a little misleading. There are a growing number of American buyers/collectors/dealers who seem to be buying, particularly abstract Delphis and Aegean wares, which has much to do with the increasing growth of Twentieth century collecting in America. Buying however is largely restricted to within America and Canada. Shipping charges are certainly something that it going to cause problems in the immediate future in terms of buying outside the UK. Supposedly items imported liable for import VAT if less than one hundred years old.

At two new Twentieth Century Fairs there was more vivid and brightly coloured Poole than there was Clarice Cliff, perhaps showing a trend for the future and certainly indicating a growing awareness of the British Pottery wares. It is interesting to speculate how much Delphis, Aegean and Atlantis there is in Japan as the Japanese were strong importers of these wares at the time. There has also been a strong Japanese following in the past for 'things' specifically related to the 1960s, the high-tech, clinical, clean lines and use of bold colouring being styles being particularly sought after, a recent example being the abstract Susie Cooper coffee set designs of the 1960s period.

It will be very interesting to see how the interest in and growth of Poole Pottery develops in the early years of the new millennium.

Further Information

The Poole Pottery Collectors Club

This is the official company Collector's Club, established in 1995, following the involvement of Richard Dennis (former Director) and Sally Tuffin (former head designer) in Poole Pottery. The resident Poole Pottery expert, Leslie Hayward, along with Gloria Peek (Club Secretary) was largely responsible for the co-ordination of the club, as well as the magazine and the various events that took place. Today there is a new club secretary, Clive Bailey, who has also been appointed Curator to the Museum, both jobs being rolled into one.

As a member of the Collector's Club you are not only given a number but an enamelled metal pin/badge in the form of a vase with a leaping stag design in the manner of the traditional form of decoration. There are three colour magazines a year, featuring articles about the past and present of Poole Pottery, new research, forthcoming and past specialist auctions, recent company news and notices of forthcoming special events and gala days. For many members one of the most important reasons for joining the club is to be able to purchase the annual members-only items, as well as the members only exclusive pieces. There is also the opportunity to buy/order limited edition wares, one-off Gala Day pieces, not to mention attending the Gala Day to bid on trials, out of stock pieces, etc. You can also get 10% off anything in the shop or the Carters restaurant, free entry to the Museum and the factory tour and your guests get in for 50% off.

Membership costs £15 (individual) or £20 (joint/overseas). How do you join or find out more about the Collector Club? Well, there is 'snail mail' and there is 'e-mail', as well as Internet and fax. The latter being found on the Collector's Club page on the Poole Pottery web site – www.poolepottery.co.uk – where you can fill in your details, credit card, address, etc, print out the page and fax it to the Club. The other way, of course, is to ask for a membership form by writing/faxing to : The Secretary, Poole Pottery Collectors Club, Poole Pottery Ltd, The Quay, Pool, Dorset. BH15 1RF. Telephone: 01202 666200, Fax: 01202 682894

This is so far the only collectors club that seems to exist, at least to my knowledge, but I would not be surprised to find one or two others developing in the near future.

Bibliography

The Poole Potteries Jennifer Hawkins, 1980.
Poole Pottery – The First Hundred Years Lucien Myers. 1973.
Poole Pottery Lesley Hayward & Paul Atterbury. 1998.
Brightening the Long Days – Hospital Tile Pictures John Greene. Tile & Architecural Ceramic Society. 1987.
Women Designing – Redefining Design in Britain Between the Wars Edited by Jill Seddon and Suzette Worden, 1994.
A Century of Art Education in the Potteries Reginald Haggar. 1953.
Centenary Exhibition 1853-1953 Stoke-on-Trent College of Art. 1953.
Denby Pottery. 1809-1997 Irene & Gordon Hopwood. 1997.
Encyclopaedia of British Art Pottery Victoria Bergsen. 1991.
Encyclopaedia of Pottery and Porcelain Elizabeth Cameron. 1986.
Ceramics Frances Hannah. 1986.
Ceramics of the 1950s Graham Mclaren. 1997.
The New Look Design in the Fifties Lesley Jackson. 1991.
20th Century Tiles Hans Van Lemmen & Chris Blanchett. 1999.
The Sixties Decorative Art Yearbooks Lesley Jackson. 1998.
Studio Yearbook 1922, 1923, 1924 and 1927.
Hints on Household Taste Charles L Eastlake. Published 1986 from the unabridged republication of the 1969 Dover edition of *Hint on Household Taste in Furniture, Upholstery and Other Details*, a republication of the 1878 publication by Longmans, Green and Co.
The House Beautiful Clarence Cook. Published 1995 from the unabridged republication by Charles Scribner's Sons, New York, 1881.

Periodicals & Catalogues

Pottery Gazette and Glass Trades Review
Pottery and Glass Record
British Industries Fair – Exhibition catalogue 1917.
British Art in Industry – Exhibition catalogue 1935.
The Art Journal 1905.
The Studio
Design
Ceramics
Glazed Expressions – Tile and Architectural Ceramic Society
The Poole Potteries – Exhibition catalogue. Victoria and Albert Museum, Jennifer Hawkins. 1979.
Poole in The 1950s – Exhibition catalogue. Richard Dennis Gallery. 1997.
Poole Pottery Studio in the 1960s – Exhibition catalogue H Lyons, R Woolley & N Boston. 1993.
The Potters of Poole – Article in Art & Antiques, Graham Crossingham-Gower, March 22nd. 1975.
Poole Pottery Poole Pottery Souvenir Guide Book. c.1996.
Poole Pottery Collectors Club magazines – 1997 to 1999.
Auction Catalogues – Sotheby's, Christie's South Kensington, Cottee's of Wareham.
Poole Pottery Archive Material

Notes

Notes

Notes

Poole Pottery
Carter & Company and their Successors, 1873-1998
Leslie Hayward
Edited by Paul Atterbury

303 x 227mm, cloth ISBN 0 903685 62 0, 192pp over 500 colour plates and numerous
illustrations in black and white, lists of marks and full index
Price £45.00

Published by Richard Dennis
The Old Chapel, Shepton Beauchamp, nr Ilminster, Somerset TA19 0LE
Telephone and Fax 01460 242009